This book has been made possible through the patronage and cooperation of the following companies and institutions:

Albany Convention and Visitors Bureau

American Museum of the Moving Image

Annette Greene Museum at The Fragrance Foundation

Astoria Development Corporation

Barneys New York

Bergdorf Goodman

Bloomingdale's

Bronx Zoo/Wildlife Conservation Society

Café Boulud

Cathedral of All Saints

Crowne Plaza La Guardia Airport

Daniel

Designer Limousines

Destination Services

Diamond District

Donald Elliot Photography

Empire State Building

Flushing Council on Culture and the Arts

Flushing Town Hall

Getaway Travel & Sightseeing Tours

Gifts Organic

Grand Central Partnership Inc.

Holiday Inn, Wall Street

Hotel Wales

Intrepid Sea, Air, Space Museum

Isamu Noguchi Garden Museum

Jamaica Bay Wildlife Refuge

Lincoln Center for the Performing Arts

Macy's Herald Square

Metropolitan Opera House

Morgan State House

Morris Berman Studio Inc.

NuJapple Marketing

NYC & Company

Oceana

On The Ave Hotel

P.S.1

Pumpkinmaternity

Queens Borough President's Office

Queens Botanical Garden

Queens Country Farm Museum

Queens Gazette

Queens Museum of Art

Queens Theater in the Park

Queens Wildlife Center

RCPI Trust

Rockaway Chamber of Commerce

Sheraton JFK Airport Hotel

Skyline Entertainment

Smithsonian National Museum of the American Indian

Socrates Sculpture Park

The Beach Club

The Excelsior

The Franklin

The Jewish Museum

The Lucerne New York

The Muse

The NBA Store

The New Yorker Ramada

The Regency

Tilles Center for the Performing Arts

Top of the World Trade Center

USTA National Tennis Center

Whitney Museum of American Art

Best of
Impressions in continuity
New York

Statue of Liberty
Photo by: © *Don Riepe*

Acknowledgements

We would like to acknowledge the General Managers of the hotels we featured for their interest and appreciation of the project.

A special thanks to Anita Duquette, Anne J. Scher, Anthony & Julia Botte, Russ Tall Chief, Daniel Boulud, Sarah Pecker, Jo Ann Jones, Nilda Apolinario Pena, Georgette Farkas, Cynthia Chung, Annette Greene, Rona Gruber, Sonia Balandra, Zita Rosenthal, Susan Agin, Liz Sulik, Mary Lapegna, Bruno & Elide Belic, Tiffani Cailor, Monica Black, Jurrian Veth, Laura Boiardi, Kathleen Pettit, Morris Berman, Ralph D'Ovidio, Kenny Varone, Michelle Vernard, George Caballero, Leon Mohall, Harvey Paul Davidson, Tess M. Cabadin, Mary & Leo Arpin for their enthusiasm and cooperation for this long and tedious endeavor.

Our sincerest gratitude to Edward Wallis Doucet. Charles Kuhtic, Luis Miguel B. Arcangel, Ryan L. Bouie, Don Riepe, Allison Caalim, Mark Brogna, Darlene Frenette & Aileen Caalim. All these people of many talents have infused their creative ideas into the project right from the beginning.

To all our corporate clients, our heartfelt appreciation for their patronage.

To our family and friends for being there for us throughout the project . We are forever grateful.

Lastly to New York, the city of Manhattan, the five boroughs - Brookyn, Bronx, Manhattan, Queens, Staten Island and the State Capital that served as an inspiration to make this book a reality.

Introduction

Probably no other place in the world has so much been written about as New York.

This book is a compendium of our best efforts to capture the history, soul and essence of all there is about New York. Visiting beyond the traditional and exploring its beautiful city, the nearby boroughs, and the State Capital.

The first five chapters have been devoted to museums, hotels, restaurants, architectural wonders, panoramic attractions, wildlife and the Peninsula known as Rockaways.

Within the pages of Best of New York *Impressions in continuity* the reader will find extraordinary visions of collections from the Whitney Museum of American Art, The Jewish Museum, The Smithsonian National Museum of the American Indian, The Annette Green Museum at The Fragrance Foundation and the Intrepid Sea, Air, Space Museum.

A body of informative materials can also be learned about the history of the Rockefeller Center, Grand Central Terminal, Empire State Building and the World Trade Center.

The readers will certainly appreciate full color photographs of animals in their natural habitat at the Bronx Zoo/Wildlife Conservation Society and the Jamaica Wildlife Refuge, a wonderland of beaches, forest trails and marshes made accessible by boardwalk, and only an hour away from the city.

We also explored Queens, its history and how it metamorphosized into a melting pot of various cultures. We tried to capture the beauty and grandeur of Albany, and its incredible architectural legacy.

Throughout the book, the choice of images richly compliments the text providing the reader with a glorious visual journey of New York.

The subject matter in the book is legion, however, we are pleased that we so far summoned the best available subjects at a given time and space to bring out the best literature possible.

This book is our humble tribute to New York from the traditions of its glorious past to its exciting present.

New York is truly a great experience.

Travel Forward to the Past

The Jewish Museum, New York
Photograph © 1993 Peter Aaron/Esto. All rights reserved.

Whitney Museum of American Art

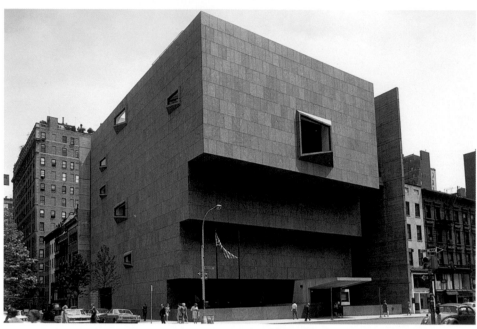

Marcel Breuer, Architect, Exterior of Whitney Museum, 1966

New York City's Whitney Museum of American Art is the leading supporter of 20th-century and contemporary American art. Located on Madison Avenue at 75th Street, the Whitney's holdings include those representing more than 1,900 artists, which total approximately 12,000 works of art. The objective of the Museum is to collect, preserve, interpret and exhibit only American artwork. Having been the first museum devoted to the work of living American artists, innovations is the work that best describes the institution.

The Whitney was founded in 1930 by sculptor Gertrude Vanderbilt Whitney. She was familiar with the challenges faced by early twentieth century American artists, how it was almost impossible for them to exhibit or sell their work and new ideas. In an effort to support her fellow peers, Whitney purchased and displayed their work herself. In 1914, she instituted the Whitney Studio in Greenwich Village. The studio showed exhibits of living American artists whose works were rejected by traditional art academies. Her collection of works grew to 500 by 1929, so she submitted them with an endowment to the Metropolitan Museum of Art, who turned her down. In 1930, she decided to open her own museum that would be dedicated to presenting only American artwork. The Whitney Museum of American Art was opened in 1931 on West Eighth Street in Greenwich Village. As it grew, it moved in 1954 to an expanded site on West 54th Street and then to its present site on Madison Avenue in 1966.

Not only does the Whitney present its works at Madison Avenue, but it has also expanded its exhibitions to be displayed at a corporate funded branch facility at Philip Morris Incorporated on Park Avenue and 42nd Street, which opened in 1983. This branch facility allows the museum to increase access to its renowned collection.

The Whitney's main resource is its permanent collection, which is disputably the finest collection of twentieth century American art in the world. It started out as 600 works of art when the museum opened in 1931, but has grown to approximately 12,000 works representing more than 1,900 artists. These works include paintings, sculptures, prints, drawings and photographs. Another signature exhibition is the Biennial, which is America's only continuous series of exhibits examining the most recent developments in the country's artwork. Exhibitions at the Whitney range from historical surveys and in-depth retrospectives of major 20th-century artists to group shows introducing young or relatively unknown artists to a larger public. The museum is also the first New York museum to introduce a major exhibition of the art form of video. The New American Filmmaker Series, established in 1970, backs the work of independent, non-commercial filmmakers. The demonstration of the media as a contemporary art form is part of the museum's dedication.

For more than 70 years, the Whitney Museum of American Art has allowed artists of this country to display their works to the public even before they become well-recognized. From its conception to the present day, the museum has opened the doors for many artists to present their work to the American culture.

Joseph Stella, <u>The Brooklyn Bridge: Variation on an Old Theme</u>, 1939
Oil on Canvas
70 x 42 in. (177.8 x 106.7 cm.)
Collection of Whitney Museum of American Art
Purchase

Robert Henri
Gertrude Vanderbilt Whitney, 1916
Oil on canvas
50 x 72 in. (127 x 182.9 cm.)
Collection of Whitney Museum of American Art
Gift of Flora Whitney Miller

Elie Nadelman
Tango *ca. 1919.*
Painted cherry wood and gesso
35 7/8 x 26 x 13 7/8 in.
(91.1 x 66 x 35.2 cm.)
Collection of Whitney Museum of American Art

Reginald Marsh
Twenty Cent Movie, 1936
Egg tempera on composition board
30 x 40 in. (76.2 x 101.6 cm.)
Collection of Whitney Museum of American Art
Purchase

Willem deKooning
Woman and Bicycle, 1952-1953
Oil on Canvas
76 1/2 x 49 in. (194.3 x 124.5 cm.)
Collection of Whitney Museum of American Art
Purchase
© 2001 Willem deKooning Revocable Trust/Artists Rights Society (ARS), New York

Lee Bronson, <u>Underpass</u>.
October 29, 1999 - March17, 2000
Whitney Museum of American Art at Philip Morris
Photo by: *George Hirose*

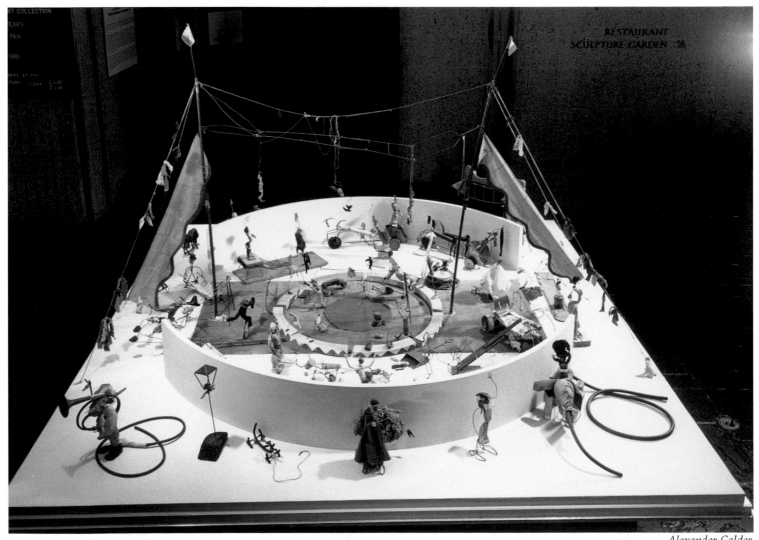

Alexander Calder
Calder's Circus, 1926 - 1931
Mixed media: wire, wood, metal, cloth, yarn,
paper, cardboard, leather, string, rubber
tubing, corks, buttons, rhinestones, pipe
cleaners, bottle caps
54 x 94 1/4 x 94 1/4 in.
(137.2 x 239.4 x 239.4 cm.)
Collection of Whitney Museum of American Art

Leonard & Evelyn Lauder Gallery
Left to Right: Robert Henri, Gaston Lachaise, Maurice Prendergast,
Robert Henri, George Bellows, Gertrude Vanderbilt Whitney

Richard Diebenkorn
<u>*Girl looking at Landscape*</u>, *1957*
Oil on canvas
59 x 60 3/8 in. (149.9 x 153.4 cm.)
Collection of Whitney Museum of American Art
Gift of Mr. and Mrs. Alan H. Temple

The Jewish Museum

The Jewish Museum, New York
Photograph © 1993 Peter Aaron/Esto. All rights reserved

The Jewish Museum is a distinguished institution committed to displaying the phenomenal scope and diversity of Jewish culture. It is one of the world's largest and most important cultural institutions, capturing 4,000 years of Jewish history through the use of authentic arts and artifacts. Located along New York City's Museum Mile, The Jewish Museum links both Jews and non-Jews to a rich body of values and traditions and provides a rare source of insight and inspiration to visitors.

Founded in 1904, the Museum's collection was housed in the library of the Jewish Theological Seminary of America. Forty years later Mrs. Frieda Schiff Warburg, widow of one of the Seminar trustees, donated the Warburg Family mansion for use as the museum. The mansion was located at 1109 Fifth Avenue where it opened to the public in 1947. The mansion had been home to the Museum ever since.

The mission of the Jewish Museum is to preserve, study and interpret Jewish cultural history. Its growing collection has grown to more than 28,000 objects. Included among the various items displayed are paintings, sculptures, works on paper, photographs, ethnographic material, archaeological artifacts, numismatics, ceremonial objects and broadcast media materials. The Museum's collections address the entire Jewish experience from biblical times to the present.

The Jewish Museum's permanent exhibition is called <u>Culture and Continuity: The Jewish Journey</u>. Containing different pieces of art, artifacts and media installations, this exhibit looks at the vital interaction between continuity and change within Jewish traditions and way of life. This permanent exhibition comprises seventeen galleries and included within the galleries is a two-story space of a recreated ancient synagogue, featuring rare and magnificent ceremonial art, an intense sculpture interpreting the Holocaust, and paintings that speak to the contemporary Jewish experience.

Special temporary exhibitions are often displayed throughout the year in the Museum. These exhibits often combine art and artifacts and interpret them through the description of social history in order to explore important ideas and topics. The exhibits range from highlights of Jewish historical events to more personal interpretations of Jewish culture by renowned contemporary artists. Such artists include Robert Rauschenberg, Helen Frankenthaler and others.

Over the years, the Museum expanded first in 1959 with the installation of a sculpture court alongside the Mansion, and then with the addition of the Albert A. List Building in 1963 which provided more exhibition and program space. In 1989, museum officials undertook a major renovation and expansion project, which was completed in 1993. The completion of the renovation doubled the Museum's gallery space, created new and improved shops and cafes and preserved the exterior of the original Warburg Mansion. Space for new educational programs was made, called the Edgar M. Bronfman Center for Education. At this educational center with modern classroom spaces, a family center, and children's exhibition gallery, visitors to the museum enjoy art workshops, performances and exhibits created for children and families.

The Jewish Museum offers membership to visitors. Members are privileged with offers such as free admission, invitations to exhibition previews and special events, tours with curators of exhibitions in progress and distinctive travel opportunities. Jewish Museum publications and shop discounts are also available to members.

The Jewish Museum has been a source of education, inspiration and shared human values for people of all cultures. A visit to the museum provided many with a sense of the Jewish experience, both secular and religious. Demonstrating the strength of Jewish identity and culture, the Museum offers a wide range of opportunities for exploring multiple facets of the Jewish experience and for education current and future generations.

Hanukkah Lamp, Frankfurt, 1706-32, Maker: Johann Adam Boller (1679-1732);
cast, engraved, filigree, hammered, and gilt silver; enamel plaques.
Gift of Mrs. Frieda Warburg
© The Jewish Museum, New York

Burial Plaque, Rome 3rd - 4th century CE, carved and painted marble.
Gift of Henry L. Moses in memory of Mr. and Mrs. Henry P. Goldschmidt
© The Jewish Museum, New York

Torah Crown, Lemberg (Lvov) silver: repousse, cast, cut-out, engraved, parcel-gilt; semiprecious stones; glass.
Galicia, 1764/65 and 1773.
Gift of Dr. Harry G. Friedman
© The Jewish Museum, New York

Hanukkah Lamp, Italy, 17th century: Triple Arches and Balustrade; cast and sheet-metal copper alloy; wood.
Gift of Dr. Harry G. Friedman
© The Jewish Museum, New York

Eastern Sigillata Ware Jug, Eastern Mediterranean, 1st century BCE-1st century CE, wheelturned, slipped terra-cotta
Gift of the Betty and Max Ratner Collection
© The Jewish Museum, New York

Moritz Daniel Oppenheim
The return of the Jewish Volunteer from the Wars of Liberation to His Family
Still Living in Accordance with Old Customs 1833/34 Oil on Canvas.
Gift of Richard and Beatrice Levy, the donors maintaining life rights.
© The Jewish Museum, New York

Max Weber, *The Talmudists*,
1934, oil on canvas
Gift of Mrs. Nathan Miller.
© The Jewish Museum, New York

Reuven Rubin, *Goldfish Vendor*,
1928, oil on canvas.
Gift of Kitty and Harold J. Ruttenberg
© The Jewish Museum, New York

Hanukkah Lamp, The Netherlands, 18th - 19th century: Tulip and Hearts, repousse, traced, and punched copper alloy.
Gift of Dr. Harry G. Friedman
© The Jewish Museum, New York

Smithsonian National Museum of the American Indian

The facade of historic Alexander Hamilton U.S. Custom House, permanent home of the Smithsonian National Museum of the American Indian.

The distinguished George Gustav Heye Center of the National Museum of the American Indian opened in lower New York on October 30, 1994. With 20,000 square feet of exhibition and public-access areas, it occupies two floors of the Alexander Hamilton U.S. Custom House, located on One Bowling Green in lower Manhattan. The custom house, designed by architect Cass Gilbert, has been named a National Historic Landmark as well as a New York City landmark.

The National Museum of the American Indian itself was established for the preservation, study and presentation of the life, history, culture, literature and arts of the Native Peoples of the Western Hemisphere. George Gustav Heye was founder of the museum and served as its director from its beginning until 1957. His own personal collection of Native American materials began as a hobby in 1897, and although he initially had a career in investment banking, the collection soon became his sole passion. Heye amassed the largest private collection of Native American objects in the world, one that also has become the basis of the museum's collection. In November 1989, former President George Bush signed the legislation to establish The Museum of the American Indian, Heye foundation as part of the Smithsonian Institution. Congress also established two other facilities, including a Cultural Resources Center in Suitland, Maryland and the National Museum on the National Mall in our nation's capitol.

Over the years, the museum has accumulated nearly one million objects as well as photo archives of an estimated 86,000 prints and negatives. The objects in the collection of the National Museum of the American Indian include Navajo weavings and blankets; textiles from Peru and Mexico; basketry from the Southwest; Aztec mosaics; and decorated hides and garments from the North American Plains Indians. About 70 percent come from North America and 30 percent from Central and South America.

The Heye Center in New York, which offers free admission and is open daily, currently features "All Roads Are Good: Native Voices on Life and Culture." "All Roads Are Good," 23 Native American selectors from throughout the Western Hemisphere chose more than 300 objects from the museum's collection to display for their artistic, spiritual and personal significance. Selectors who chose the objects on the basis of artistic, cultural, spiritual and personal significance, were asked to speak about the chosen objects and their responses were recorded to accompany their selections. Catalogue is available in the museum shop for $29.95.

Jolene Rickard, Reservation X

Beauty, Honor, and Tradition: The Legacy of Plains Indian Shirts (Dec. 10, 2000 - Nov. 4, 2001), featuring 50 visually stunning and spiritually powerful Plains Indian shirts from the museum's collection, explores the beauty, power, history, iconography, construction and materials of Plains Indian shirts from the 19th and 20th centuries. Curated by George Horse Capture (Gros Ventre), NMAI's Deputy Asst. Director of Cultural Resources, and his son, Joe Horse Capture, the exhibition is presented in collaboration with the Minneapolis Institute of Arts. Catalogue is available for $39.95.

Seth Eastman Watercolors: A Soldier Artist Among the Dakota (April 5 - Oct. 7, 2001) features 56 watercolor paintings from the W. Duncan MacMillan collection — some never before on public display. The works are considered some of the most important visual records of everyday Dakota life in Minnesota during the mid-19th century. Eastman was the leading pictorial historian of Native Americans in the 19th century and a career army officer assigned to frontier duty at Fort Snelling. Catalogue is available in the museum shop for $14.95.

Spirit Capture: Native Americans and the Photographic Image, on view July 21, 2001 - 2002, explores the meaning of photographic images of and by Native Americans in order to communicate Native perspectives on the cultural history and experiences of Native peoples during the past 150 years. Photographer, subject, and viewer are considered as the exhibition seeks to privilege the understandings of the people in the photographs, while examining the roles and motives of those who created the images. Drawing upon NMAI's Photo Archive of approximately 125,000 images, the exhibition was curated by Richard W. Hill, Sr. (Tuscarora) and Natasha Bonilla-Martinez. Catalogue is available in the museum shop for $29.95.

In addition to inaugural exhibitions, the Heye Center also features temporary presentations as well as public programs. In addition, the museum's Film and Video presents daily film, video and radio programs from Native media organizations from the Americas, in addition to special programs for children.

C. Maxx Stevens, Reservation X

Marianne Nicolson, *Reservation X*

Mary Longman, Reservation X

Seed Gathering Basket, Hupa, Ca

Shelly Niro, Reservation X

Cradleboard, Yuma, Az

F. Kabotie, Hopi, Snake Dance

Bark Mask, Tierra del Fuego

INTREPID

SEA · AIR · SPACE · MUSEUM

For 31 years USS INTREPID served in the defense of the United States. She survived bombs, torpedoes and kamikazes, performed as NASA Prime Recovery Vessel and as the US Navy and Marine Corps Bicentennial Exposition Vessel.

She operated in every corner of the globe, sailing millions of miles during her career. Most of her life was dedicated to keeping the peace and preventing war. Yet, when she was called upon-she served admirably during both World War Two and Vietnam.

INTREPID's national significance is unparalleled as a Museum, permanently moored in the center of the country's most populous region, she's readily accessible to 40 million Americans and millions of foreign visitors. Resting peacefully in New York Harbor, the memory of her deeds and echoes of her crew are but gentle whispers as she embarks on her new mission.

Once aboard the "Fighting I", visitors walk upon hallowed decks comparable to the national historic sites at Gettysburgh and Valley Forge.

The INTREPID SEA • AIR • SPACE • MUSEUM complex has three major components, the aircraft carrier INTREPID, the submarine GROWLER and the destroyer EDSON, all berthed at Pier 86 on the Hudson River in Manhattan. As you will soon discover, the Intrepid Museum is more than a collection of historic ships. It is a floating exploration center and launchpad into a world of sea, air and space technology.

The INTREPID SEA • AIR • SPACE • MUSEUM is run by a private, not-for-profit educational foundation dedicated to the preservation of American history. It is not part of the U.S. Navy or any branch of the Federal Government. Admission prices pay for less than one third of the operating budget of the complex.

Visitor amenities are located throughout the museum complex for your convenience. The information Desk is in Navy Hall, directly across from the main entrance at Tower 2. At the Information Desk, museum personnel can direct you to the location of exhibits, special events, services and routes to the flight deck and bridge. Meals and snacks are available in the Stars and Stripes Cafe located at the

ship's stern near the far end of Technologies Hall. A refreshment area is located on the second floor of the Visitors Center. Restrooms are on both levels of the Visitors Center and at the far end of Technologies Hall. Public telephones are available next to the entrance at the top of Tower 3 in Pioneer Hall and at the starboard side entrance to the Fantail onboard the INTREPID.

Self-guided tours of INTREPID average between one and four hours depending on the time of year, day of the week or your interest in specific exhibits. The Acoustiguide audio program enables you to tour INTREPID at your own pace. The EDSON and the GROWLER provide complimentary guided tours. For optimum viewing, museum management recommends you tour the submarine GROWLER at the beginning of your visit.

The Museum Store opens daily at 10:00 a.m. and is located in the Box Office building's outer area. The Museum Store offers a wide range of items from military clothing and gear to souvenirs, toys, books and videos for patriots of all ages. Be sure to check out the Intrepid Museum website for online purchases.

Children at controls

Intrepid Museum

Annette Green Museum at The Fragrance Foundation

*I*n November of 1999, the Annette Green Museum at The Fragrance Foundation, the first fragrance museum in the United States, opened its doors to the public. Created to expand the awareness, enjoyment and appreciation of fragrance, its imagery and role in people's lives throughout history, the Museum is the first of its kind devoted solely to the joys and pleasures of the senses of smell, sight and touch.

The Museum was conceived by Annette Green, President of The Fragrance Foundation, for whom the Museum is named. She is recognized as one of America's leading fragrance authorities and futurists and has been associated with The Fragrance Foundation, the non-profit, educational arm of the international fragrance industry for the past 40 years. Under the guidance of Ms. Green, The Fragrance Foundation has become the central source of educational, historical and cultural information. She has created a wide range of symposia and instituted an extensive research library of publications including one of her own. Annette Green, with co-author Linda Dyett wrote the fascinating coffee table book, *The Secrets of Aromatic Jewelry* (Flammarion), which is the only book to explore the glamorous history of jewelry which has held fragrance.

Celebrating 50 Years of Fragrance in America was the exhibit that opened the Museum. It was an extraordinary documentation of fragrance as an essential component in defining the museum and its mission through a historic fifty-year tour of memory and emotion. The exhibit proudly showcased the Museum's first acquisitions - an exquisite Erte sculpture entitled, "Perfume," 18th Century Adams Cabinets and a timeline that visually encapsulated 50 years of scent &

society. The Museum's unique Smelling Scenter allowed Museum-goers an interactive experience by smelling fragrances from all five decades.

The second exhibit at the Annette Green Museum at The Fragrance Foundation opened June 7th, 2000 during "FiFi" week and was dedicated to the industry's most prestigious Awards, the "FiFi's." In 1972, Annette Green created the "FiFi" Awards, the 'Oscars' of the Fragrance Industry, designed to honor the extraordinary creativity of the international fragrance industry in America. The American "FiFi" Awards are celebrating their 29th year in 2001.

This exhibit saluted **FAB "FIFI" NIGHTS: The stars! The "FiFi" Awards! The Winning Scent-sations!** - as a tribute to "FiFi" winners, the celebrity presenters and the glamour of the award ceremony. A "Stairway to the Stars" was erected featuring a tower of factices of "FiFi" Award winners. Miniature versions of five grand stage sets by designer, Davie Lerner, used for the "FiFi" Ceremonies at Avery Fisher Hall, Lincoln Center for the Performing Arts over the years were on view. The Museum's "Smelling Scenter" invited visitors to experience the Award-winning fragrances.

The critically-acclaimed Museum's third success was **"Gents Scents: "The Male Fragrance Adventure - Century to Century"** which opened November 9, 2000 during National Fragrance Week. This exhibit was the *first* to feature a historic journey through the world of male fragrances and their societal impact from the 17th Century and the Napoleonic era to the present.

"At a time in men's lives when fragrance enjoyment has reached new heights, "Gents Scents" offered a unique

Stairway of "FiFi" Award winning fragrance factices

sociological, psychological and sometimes whimsical tour of the sensory world men have made their own" said Annette Green. "Not since Napoleon considered fragrance his absolute wartime essential has scent become such a symbol of masculinity."

GENTS SCENTS featured a unique "hat tree" showcasing 33 historic hats and headwear from the 1700's to the present, as well as a turn-of-the-century Koken barber chair, a traveling tortoise shell grooming case ca. 1900 and, of course, an historical overview of men's fragrances. Over 300 rare and never-before-seen pieces were in the exhibition.

The Fourth exhibition opening on June 6, 2001 is a real newsmaker! The exhibition, Sex, Scents and Cinema, will explore what makes scents so irresistible to our significant others. In real life and in the reel life of the cinema, lovers have been drawn to one another by the mystery, allure and romance of fragrance. The scentual appeal of fragrance is the centerpiece of the lot when the **Annette Green Museum** opens this exciting new exhibit featuring film-clips, stills and according to public opinion - the sexiest fragrances.

In conjunction with the exhibition, The Fragrance Foundation is launching a nationwide survey on its website. **The public will be invited to answer two questions: "What's the sexiest fragrance you have ever worn?" ("What's the sexiest fragrance your significant other has ever worn?")** Once the responses are tabulated, the fragrances receiving the most votes will be featured in the exhibition. Memberships in the museum are available in seven categories. Special membership activities include lecture series, invitations to exclusive previews and receptions, presentations by leading curators, collectors, and/or

conservators of fragrance art, object days featuring in-depth discussions about selected pieces from your personal fragrance collection followed by a reception, tours of perfumery labs (meet a perfumer).

The Fragrance Foundation is the non-profit, educational arm of the international fragrance industry. It was founded in 1949 by a group of industry leaders. Membership categories include: Active (Manufacturers and Suppliers), Associate (Media, Advertising and Marketing Agencies, Financial Service Firms, Consultants, Package Designers, etc.) and Retailers. Located at 145 East 32nd Street, the purpose of The Fragrance Foundation as stated in the By-Laws, is to encourage the enjoyment of fragrance in all its many forms through the dissemination of information on the manufacture, application and care of such products; to obtain educational materials and distribute such information to inspire a keener interest among all peoples in the positive role of the sense of smell and fragrance in their lives globally.

The Foundation serves the international fragrance industry, retail, media, students, libraries, etc., as well as the public, providing them with a central source for educational and historical information on all aspects of fragrance and the sense of smell. A comprehensive library is maintained for use by members, students and media which encompasses a collection of current books, videos, audiotapes and articles on fragrance as well as historical books and manuscripts. A newly-designed conference centre with state of the art, audiovisual equipment is available for bookings by member companies and includes museum visits with docents.

Chess Set

*32 piece set is composed of colognes Wild Country, Tai Winds,
Avon Spicy, Oland, Tai Winds and Deep Woods colognes. The
original set have silver tops and amber bodies, the second
(opposing) set, vice versa.*
Avon, 1971-1978

*A 32 piece chess set was Avon's Choice in 1971-1978 for a
collection of their men's colognes, aftershaves and hair lotions.*

Erte sculpture "Perfume" - gift of Givaudan

18th Century Adams Cabinet - gift of Elizabeth Arden

Exhibition case featuring historic and modern men's scent bottles

*A Koken "turn of the century" barber's chair
and dressing/shaving table with mirror*

*A hat-tree sprouts giant men's fragrance factices and period
hats setting the chronology of the "Gents Scents" exhibition*

Giant fragrance bottles used for display called factices.

Exhibition focal point - November 2000

Landmarks and Architectural Wonders

Grand Central Terminal's "Classical" Facade

Grand Central Terminal

Grand Central Terminal's "Classical" Facade

*I*magine Park Avenue from 45th to 49th Street as a rail yard a corridor of smoke and cinders extending uptown from 49th Street. Think of breweries and factories operating where the Waldorf-Astoria, Lever House and the Seagram Building now stand. Picture to the east a district of tenements, warehouses, and slaughterhouses. In place of the United Nations and Tudor City, the squatters' shacks of Dutch Hill, inhabited by paupers, criminal gangs, and a herd of goats. It is hard to conceive that this cityscape ever existed, let alone that is was the environment in which Grand Central Terminal took shape less than one hundred years ago.

While Grand Central Terminal stands today as one of New York City's most famous landmarks, it was by no means the first railroad station in New York City. In fact, the current structure is neither the first to claim the name "Grand Central," or to occupy the present location at 42nd and Park. Yet, the story of Grand Central Terminal allows one to gaze back and observe much of the history of the City of New York, and to witness the growth of a vibrant metropolis reflected in an unrivaled monument of civic architecture.

The first rail line into New York City the New York and Harlem Railroad-was formed in 1831 and began service to a terminal at Fourth

Avenue and 23rd Street the following year. Over the next five years, the railroad constructed a station, offices, and stables (horses pulled the trains where engines could not go) along the Fourth (Park) Avenue, at 26th and 27th Streets, through subsequent expansion and reconstruction, the New York and Harlem Railroad Station would come to occupy the entire block bounded by Fourth and Madison Avenues and 26th and 27th Streets. (In 1871, P.T. Barnum purchased the New York and Harlem Railroad Station and converted it into Madison Square Garden the first of several structures to bear that historic name.)

Shipping magnate "Commodore" Cornelius Vanderbilt acquired the Hudson River Railroad in 1864. Soon after, Vanderbilt added the New York Central Railroad (at that time only a link between Albany and Buffalo) to his holdings and consolidated his position by creating a link between Spuyten Duyvil and Mott Haven, allowing Hudson River trains to arrive at a common East Side terminal. In 1869, Vanderbilt purchased property between 42nd and 48th Streets, Lexington and Madison Avenue for construction of a new train depot and rail yard. On this site would rise the first Grand Central.

Constructed of glass and steel, the 100-foot wide by 650-foot long structure rivaled the Eiffel Tower and Crystal Palace for primacy as the most

dramatic engineering achievement of the 19th century. The updated station also featured a "classical" facade, a unified 16,000 square-foot waiting room, and distinctive ornamentation, including monumental cast-iron eagles with wingspans of 13 feet. (In fact, one these eagles was recently salvaged and will rise again above Grand Central Terminals new entrance at 43rd Street and Lexington Avenue).

In 1903, a select group of architects were invited to submit designs for the new Grand Central Terminal in a competition. The winning submission, was from the St. Paul firm of Reed and Stem. Subsequent to the competition, New York architects Warren and Wetmore presented the selection committee with their own proposal for the terminal. In February 1904, Warren and Wetmore and Reed and Stem entered an agreement to act as The Associated Architects of Grand Central Terminal. Construction would last ten years. Initially, trains continued to use the old Grand Central, which was eventually razed in 1910. A temporary station in the Grand Central Palace at Lexington Avenue and 43rd Street was used until 1912. Grand Central Terminal officially opened to great fanfare at 12:01 am on Sunday, February 2, 1913, and more than 150,000 people visited the new terminal on its opening day. Grand Central Terminal had arrived and New York City would never be the same again.

Grand Central Terminal is considered one of the most dramatic engineering achievements of the 19th century

Pedestrians inside Grand Central Terminal

Unrivaled monument of civic architecture

Empire State Building

Empire State Building at Sunset

For the better part of a century, most first-time visitors to New York have headed straight for the Empire State Building for the thrill of a lifetime: the journey aloft to its fabled Observatory nearly a quarter of a mile above Fifth Avenue. Here they are treated to breath-taking panoramas that embrace not only New York City, but fan out to the several surrounding states and into the far reaches of the Atlantic.

Arguably the most famous structure built by modern man, the 1,454-foot (443 meters) Empire State Building has dominated the New York City skyline since its much-heralded completion in 1931. And the story of how this modern Wonder of the World came to be is a true reflection of the American spirit.

"How high can you make it, so it won't fall down?" John Jacob Raskob, the visionary who conceived the Empire State Building asked William Lamb, the brilliant, courageous architect, in 1928. Lamb's bold answer changed history.

Raskob, a savvy Wall Street financier, had helped turn General Motors into an automotive giant and sparked the phenomenal growth of the DuPont family investment firm. To realize his crowning achievement, Raskob formed an inspired partnership with Alfred E. Smith, the former Governor of New York State and recently-defeated Democratic candidate for President of the United States. Neither man was trained as a construction engineer, architect, urban planner or real estate developer, but they knew how to get things done.

Capitalizing on Smith's New York connections and flair for showmanship, and Raskob's financial and managerial genius, within months these dynamos amassed $41 million and the necessary brains and manpower to launch the most ambitious architectural undertaking in the annals of the western world.

On May 1,1931 - just one year and forty-five days later - an astounded assemblage of dignitaries watched as Smith's grandchildren put scissors to ribbon, opening the world's tallest skyscraper, an icon that endures as New York's proudest achievement of the 20th Century.

Though now surpassed in height, the building remains unchallenged as America's must imposing National Historic Landmark. It has been featured in hundreds of films viewed by millions of movie-goers around the globe, making it beyond a doubt the best-known skyscraper in the world. With nearly 4 million visitors flowing through its hallowed halls every year, that reputation continues to soar. It is fitting that the most famous building of the 20th century has been visited by many of its most famous people - from President Franklin D. Roosevelt, Winston Churchill, countless kings, queens and heads of state to entertainment icons like Paul McCartney, and, of course, the legendary King Kong himself!

Whisked skyward aboard express elevators, visitors reach the 86th floor in less than a minute! Located 1,050 feet (320 meters) above the City's bustling streets, the Observatory offers panoramic views both from within a glass-enclosed pavilion, and from the surrounding open-air promenade. Here, in addition to the limitless vistas far into the distance, on-site high-powered binoculars can zoom in on countless attractions studding Manhattan's exciting landscape. Nothing can equal the thrilling sense of oneness with the City to be experienced from the 86th floor outdoor balcony where the only roof is the sky itself.

At 1,250 feet (381 meters) a small, fully-enclosed circular tower provides even broader vistas. From this lofty site, on the clearest days some claim to have glimpsed four neighboring states, as well as the snowwhite plumes of ocean liners plying the sea lanes over 50 miles away!

One of the most breath-taking spectacles of a lifetime awaits the night-time visitor to the open-air 86th floor Observatory. By day, one thrills to the endless expanse of geography. But by night, one is simply mesmerized by the sparkling array of stars and flickering lights scattered across the sky like a galaxy of diamonds on black velvet.

From all over the city and far beyond, the building is a light show unto itself: from sunset til midnight the top 30 floors are aglow in a rainbow of colors, keyed to a variety of special events. Visible from 80 miles around, the silhouette of the lighted tower is a virtual magnet to the eyes, beaming colored combinations of light on U.S. National Holidays (Red, White & Blue), St. Valentine's Day (Red), St. Patrick's Day (Green), United Nations Day (Blue & White), from Halloween to Thanksgiving Day (Red & Yellow), Hannukah (Blue) and the Christmas Holiday Season (Red & Green), to name but a few.

The most famous structure built by modern man

Rockefeller Center

A look from the bottom
Photo by: *Bart Barlow/RCPI Trust©*

*I*t's been called the city-within-a-city. the nation's preeminent urban complex, a welcome oasis, and the city's unofficial village green.

It's Rockefeller Center, the world's largest privately owned business and entertainment center - 19 buildings on 22 acres in the heart of midtown Manhattan.

Rockefeller Center houses more than 14 million square feet of offices and half a million square feet of retail space in the heart of New York City. The Center, founded by John D. Rockefeller, Jr. in the 1930's, was the first real estate project in the world to encompass office, retail, entertainment, and restaurants in one integrated development.

An internationally recognized symbol of New York, Rockefeller Center is the quintessential example of Art Deco style. Major works by 30 of this century's outstanding artists grace the foyers, facades, gardens and outdoor parks, making the Center one of the world's largest indoor/outdoor "museums."

In unanimously voting to bestow landmark status upon Rockefeller Center, the New York City Landmarks Preservation Commission referred to the Center as "the heart of New York . . . a great unifying presence in the chaotic core of midtown, Manhattan." Rockefeller Center is at the nucleus of the most vital concentration of retail, restaurant, corporate, and entertainment activities in this country and perhaps even the world. It is home to America's giants of business and industry trend-setting designers, time-honored retailers, and respected restaurateurs.

The present Rockefeller Center was pasture land until early in the 19th century. It was part of Manhattan's "common lands," which stretched northward some four miles from what is now 23rd Street. In 1801, Dr. David Hosack, famous New York City physician and educator bought 20 acres of these public holdings and transformed them into the famed Elgin Botanic Gardens, which he kept until 1811 when rising costs made the private venture impractical and he sold the property to New York State. Three years later, the State Legislature, under an aid-to-education act, conveyed the former Hosack land to Columbia College, today known as Columbia University.

It was October, 1928 when John D. Rockefeller, Jr., spearheading a civic drive to give New York City a new opera house, agreed to lease from Columbia University the land on which part of Rockefeller Center now stands. The plan for the new venture called for the central portion of the plot to be made available to the Metropolitan Opera Company for the erection of a new opera house, while the remainder of the land was to be leased to private builders for commercial development.

Back in 1929 however, Mr. Rockefeller found himself with a long-term annual lease commitment of 3.8 million and no opera project. The Metropolitan, plagued by legal difficulties and the Depression, abandoned its hopes for a new opera house. That left Mr. Rockefeller with a difficult decision - to abandon the site or develop it alone. He chose to build.

The result was a business and entertainment complex far in advance of its period. It had long been the ambition of far-sighted architects and real estate men to develop a large plot for business purposes in the heart of Manhattan under conditions that could utilize fully these three essentials: light, air and transportation. The spreading acres of the proposed midtown development offered this rare opportunity and the Center's original, architects - Reinhard & Hofmeister Corbett. Harrison and MacMurray; and Hood and Fouilhoux - rose brilliant to the challenge. This pioneering three-dimensional approach to urban design. with skyscrapers planned in relation to one another, to the open space, and to the Concourse area, has served as the prototype for similar developments around the world.

Rockefeller Center's 19 skyscrapers comprise a "city-within-a-city". Each building has an established relationship to the others. The, 70-story 30 Rockefeller Plaza skyscraper is the central structure in the group. Nearly one-fourth of the Center's land has been left vacant to permit the proper play of light and air and to facilitate the flow of traffic.

High on the list of visitor magnets is the Center's colorful Lower Plaza. Though a comparatively small area in a big development the Lower Plaza is probably responsible for the refashioning of more real estate complexes in the image of Rockefeller Center than any other single facet of its design. The Plaza is a rectangular reservoir of light and air in a skyscraper canyon. Once called the "quintessence of city space" by an architectural critic, it is the setting for ice skating in the winter and alfresco dining in the summer. Over the years it has drawn millions of people into the Center and has served as an effective traffic sorter for the offices and lobbies, shops and restaurants which surround its periphery. The annual arrival here of the most beautiful tree in the world overlooking the Lower Plaza signals the start of the Christmas season in Manhattan. Rockefeller Center truly is a New York landmark.

The Rockefeller Center is the quintessential example of art deco style
Photo by: *Bart Barlow/©RCPI Trust*

Rockefeller Christmas Tree
Photo by: *Bart Barlow/©RCPI Trust*

Christmas 1999
Photo by: *Bart Barlow/©RCPI Trust*

Top of the World Trade Center

New York Skyline

The World Trade Center, designed by renowned architect Minoru Yamasaki, is a virtual city within a city. Owned and operated by the Port Authority of New York and New Jersey, the Center was constructed as a bi-state headquarters for international trade. It consists of two 110-story office towers, three nine-story office buildings, the 22-story Marriott hotel and a 47-story office building.

Encompassing 11.1 million square feet of rentable office space, The World Trade Center brings together over 350 business and governmental agencies involved in marketing, financing, processing, insuring, documenting and transporting international trade. It also houses government and business firms that represent more than 30 different nations. Everyday, the Center's average daily population includes 40,000 workers and another 80,000 business and leisure visitors.

New York's distinguished World Trade Center stretches 16 acres across lower Manhattan and has become one of the most popular tourist sites in the city. One and Two World Trade Center, the landmark Twin Towers, each climb to a breathtaking 1,377 feet. The "Top of the World" Trade Center Observatory, located at Two World Trade Center, is one of the City's Most spectacular attractions, garnering an estimated two million visitors annually. The tower's two main elevators, traveling about 20 miles an hour, carry visitors to the Deck's location on the 107th floor in less than a minute. Surrounded by 232 viewing windows, the glass-enclosed Observatory offers a dramatic view in all directions, while multi-lingual monitors cite interesting places and facts. Besides the view, one can also enjoy browsing the scale models of New York City and taking a simulated helicopter ride over Manhattan, as well as souvenir shopping and fun dining.

Just a few stories higher is the World's Highest Rooftop Promenade, located above the 110th floor at 1,377 feet. Eleven feet wide, the Promenade is elevated 12 feet above the rooftop and set back 31 feet from the edge of the tower. This outdoor deck is perfect for an open-air view of the city from all sides, from the Brooklyn Bridge to the east, the Pulaski Skyway to the west, the Empire State Building to the north, and Ellis Island to the south.

One World Trade Center offers an equally impressive appeal as well, following a $25 million renovation. Windows on the World, owned by Joe Baum, is a popular restaurant located on the 107th floor. In the glass-enclosed, 240-seat dining room, one can experience a delicious meal along with a view of the city. Guests can also enjoy drinks at the famed Greatest Bar on Earth, located on the same floor.

For those seeking amusement more closer to the ground, the World Trade Center is built around the five-acre landscaped Austin J. Tobin Plaza, a park-like location that provide free summer entertainment and is New York City's largest public plaza. Directly below it is The Mall, Lower Manhattan's largest enclosed shopping center, where visitors can find a wide range of over 50 specialty shops and restaurants. The Mall is the main interior pedestrian circulation level for the entire Center. Since its dedication on April 1973, the World Trade Center has not only become a primary location for international business but a favorite place for tourists and visitors as well.

View of New Jersey

View of Statue of Liberty

View of The Towers

View of Ships

Premier Concert Halls

A night at the opera

Lincoln Center for the Performing Arts

*L*incoln Center for the Performing Arts, the foremost performing arts complex of its kind anywhere in the world, is situated on 16 acres on New York City's upper west side and made up of twelve performing arts companies and educational institutions dedicated to the arts of music, dance, and drama.

Lincoln Center for the Performing Arts welcomes some five million people into its theaters and outdoor performance spaces each year. In addition, another 100 million worldwide are part of the Lincoln Center audience through its television and radio presentations, recordings, videos, constituent tours, education programs, and outreach activities.

The concept of a single complex where groups of divergent cultural disciplines could flourish side by side came about as a result of a unique concurrence of events in New York city during the 1950s. Both the New York Philharmonic and Metropolitan Opera Company were looking for homes. At the same time, the opportunity was ripe for the revitalization of a large tract of real estate on Manhattan's upper west side.

A group of visionaries - among them John D. Rockefeller 3rd, Mayor Robert Wagner, urban planner Robert Moses, and architects Max Abramovitz, Pictro Belluschi, Wallace K. Harrison, Philip Johnson, and Eero Saarinen, along with a host of other experts in the arts, architecture, real estate, finance, education, city planning, fund raising and other areas - combined their talents and resources to shape and implement the plan.

On a clear morning on May 14, 1959, Lincoln Center for the Performing Arts became a reality when President Dwight D. Eisenhower made a trip to the two-block site on Manhattan's upper west side to turn a shovel of earth. As he dug the shovel into the ground, Leonard Bernstein gave a downbeat, and the New York Philharmonic and the Julliard Chorus broke into the Hallelujah Chorus. It was a groundbreaking in both the literal and the symbolic senses, signifying the birth of Lincoln Center for the Performing Arts and the establishment of the first cultural center of its kind.

The first building in the complex to be completed was Philharmonic Hall, and on September 23, 1962, Lincoln Center for the Performing Arts made history with a gala opening night concert by Leonard Bernstein and the New York Philharmonic. An audience of more than 3,000 people including many luminaries of the day in full evening dress filled the hall, while another 26 million watched the spectacle on TV.

Many people have speculated on how Lincoln Center got its name. It's a bit of a mystery. The neighborhood had always been known as Lincoln Square and it had been home to the Loews Lincoln Square Theater and the Lincoln Square Arcade, which also contained dance schools and studios for financially strapped artists. The Arcade was located where the Julliard School now stands. It is unlikely that the area was named for Abraham Lincoln, as there are no records or newspaper articles documenting the fact.

Today, twelve constituent companies - many the Americans flagships for the disciplines they represent - call Lincoln Center for the Performing Arts home.

1. Lincoln Center for the Performing Arts
2. The Metropolitan Opera
3. New York Philharmonic
4. The Julliard School
5. New York City of Ballet
6. New York City Opera
7. The Film Society of Lincoln Center
8. The Chamber Music Society of Lincoln Center
9. Lincoln Center Theater
10. School of American Ballet
11. The New York Public Library for the Performing Arts
12. Jazz at Lincoln Center

In January 2001, a new not-for-profit corporation, the Lincoln Center Constituent Development Project Inc., was established to implement and oversee the comprehensive reconstruction, renovation and modernization of Lincoln Center for the Performing Arts.

Metropolitan Opera House

A night at the opera

The original Metropolitan Opera House was built by a group of New York industrialists and socially prominent families as a competing opera house to the Academy of Music on Fourteenth Street. The original founders, among whom were the Vanderbilt, Morgan and Astor families, owned the building of the "old" Met and retained the use of the box seats for themselves. They then rented the house to an impresario or entrepreneurial group who actually assembled a performing company and produced opera there. This arrangement was changed several times, most notably in 1933 when the Metropolitan Opera Association was formed as a not-for-profit opera presenter. The Association bought the opera house from the box holders in 1940.

The first performance given by the Metropolitan Opera was Gounod's "Faust" on October 22, 1883, with a cast that included Christine Nilsson, Italo Campanini, Giuseppe Del Puente and Franco Novara, conducted by Auguste Vianesi. This performance took place at the original Metropolitan Opera House, located at 1423 Broadway, between 39th and 40th Streets in Manhattan.

The last opera performed at the old Metropolitan Opera House was "La Boheme" on the afternoon of April 16, 1966, followed by a Gala in the evening which featured many world renowned singers both past and current. However, the last performance at the old Met featured the Bolshoi Ballet on the closing night of their engagement on May 8, 1966.

The current Metropolitan Opera House is part of the Lincoln Center for the Performing Arts, and is owned by that institution. It is leased for 99 years to the Metropolitan Opera Association.

The Met has two major programs that foster new talent. The Lindermann Young Artist Development Program provides intensive preparation for up to three years for a limited number of artists who are between the conservatory and professional stages of a career. Second, the Metropolitan Opera National Council sponsors annual auditions in 65 districts where they hear as many as 2,000 singers from whom semi-finalists and finalists are chosen to compete on the Met stage in a Grand Finals Concert accompanied by the Metropolitan Opera Orchestra.

Franz Leár's <u>The Merry Widow</u> has its Metropolitan Opera premiere on February 17, 2000.
Pictured above is one of Antony McDonald's set models for the opera.
***Photo by:** Metropolitan Opera Technical Department*

Tristan   *Isolde*   *King Marke*
The Metropolitan Opera's new production of <u>Tristan und Isolde</u>

Scene from Leoncavallo's "Pagliacci"

Scene from Strauss' "Der Rosenkavalier"

TILLES CENTER
FOR THE PERFORMING ARTS

*T*illes Center for the Performing Arts, on the C.W. Post campus of Long Island University in Brookville, is Long Island's premier concert hall. Headed by Executive Director Elliott Sroka, it begins its 20th Anniversary season in 2000-2001. Tilles Center presents over 70 events each season in music, dance and theater, featuring world-renowned artists. The Center is also the theatrical home for many of Long Island's leading arts organizations, including the Long Island Philharmonic.

Among the artists and organizations that have been presented by the Center are the New York Philharmonic conducted by Kurt Masur, violinist Itzhak Perlman, the Big Apple Circus, Alvin Ailey American Dance Theater, New York City Opera National Company, Andrea Marcovicci, the Paper Bag Players, Wynton Marsalis, the MET Orchestra with James Levine and Patti LuPone.

Tilles Center, a part of Long Island University, has a 2,242-seat main hall and a 490-seat, more intimate Hillwood Recital Hall. The smaller theater features chamber music, cabaret, solo recitals, and theater productions for children and adults.

"The Dome" at C. W. Post was an active venue for both classical and popular music in the 1970's, featuring some of the hottest groups of the time, from Jefferson Starship to the Beach Boys. Bruce Springsteen's "Santa Claus Is Coming to Town" was recorded live from the stage of "The Dome."

In 1977 "The Dome" collapsed during a snowstorm. University officials, encouraged by wide public support and a Challenge grant from the NEA, opted to replace "The Dome" with an acoustically superior auditorium which opened in the fall of 1981 with a concert by Zubin Mehta and the New York Philharmonic. The Philharmonic was to become a cornerstone for the hall's top-notch classical programming. Following a major endowment gift from developer Gilbert Tilles and his wife Rose, the hall was renamed in their honor in 1985.

An ambitious period of expansion followed. Popular music, dance, opera and children's programs widened the Center's reach. Beginning in 1988, annual spring visits of the Big Apple Circus were hosted on the beautiful Post Campus by Tilles Center. "Music at Hillwood," featuring chamber music with commentary debuted with the support of The New York Times in the late 1980's, followed soon after by the popular "Cabaret at Club T" cabaret series in the intimate Hillwood Recital Hall.

In more recent seasons, "Reckson Jazz at Tilles" has brought exciting contemporary sounds to the Island, and "WorldStage" has offered glimpses of cultural traditions spanning the centuries and the globe. Today, Tilles Center is widely regarded as Long Island's pre-eminent not-for-profit presenter, and as a major player in the cultural life of the New York metropolitan area.

Tilles Center for the Performing Arts

Andrea Marcovicci
Tilles Center's First Lady of Cabaret - crowning,
as always, the theater with another new show.

An Evening with Marvin Hamlisch
In his first appearance since the sensational Gala XVII Gershwin
Centennial, Long Island's favorite composer/conductor/pianist,
backed by a vibrant 16-piece ensemble, opens the season.

Ballet Folklórico de México
Mexico's foremost folk ensemble for almost 50 years features 75 lavishly costumed dancers, musicians and singers. The vast quilt of Mexican cultures explodes onstage with passion and virtuosity.

Billy Taylor Trio: "What is Jazz?"
America's leading jazz educator (regularly seen on "CBS Sunday Morning")
dynamically involves young audiences in "America's classical music."

Handel's "Messiah" - Conducted by Richard Westenburg
The Musica Sacra Chorus and Orchestra has been acclaimed for over 30 years as the finest ensemble performing Handel's masterpiece.

Alvin Ailey American Dance Theater
The internationally acclaimed cultural ambassadors of dance return regularly to Tilles Center.

Billy Jonas and the Bucket Brigade
Sing, dance and bang along with folk songwriter Billy Jonas, and his collection of instruments made from found and recycled objects.

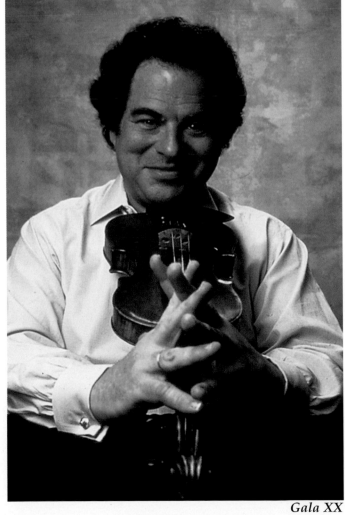

Gala XX
For GalaXX, Violinist Itzhak Perlman was guest artist with the mostly Mozart Festival Orchestra, conducted by Gerard Schwarz.

Elegance and Comfort

The Grand Suite of The Regency

THE REGENCY
A LOEWS HOTEL
NEW YORK CITY

*T*he Regency Hotel, flagship property of Loews Hotels, is known as the East Coast home to the entertainment industry and birthplace of the "Power Breakfast." Located on the Upper East Side of the Park Avenue neighborhood, it is close to the elegant boutiques on Madison and Fifth Avenue and just around the corner from Central Park. The hotel is 15 miles from LaGuardia Airport and just blocks away from Grand Central Station.

With a recent renovation in April 1999, by interior designer Connie Beale, The Regency Hotel now features 351 guestrooms including 87 suites, 540 Park Restaurant, The Library and its lobby.

Comfortably elegant accommodations feature guest rooms accented with rich materials such as silk and velvet. The beds are covered with cozy goose down comforters, spacious bathrooms feature every amenity needed and each room features its own home office with a fax machine, copier, two dedicated phone lines, voice mail and data ports for computer hookup.

Six new one-bedroom suites were designed from 12 smaller rooms. Just like Park Avenue apartments, these suites feature two full baths with new Italian marble, walk-in kitchenette, large living room area and dining room table.

Ten grand suites also were designed in four distinctive schemes symbolizing different sections of New York City. Park Avenue connotates a more traditional decor, the West Side is more romantic, the East Side is a mix of traditional and contemporary and Soho is more fun and whimsical but sophisticated and contemporary.

Located on what has become regarded as restaurant row, The Regency Hotel holds its own with the 540 Park Restaurant, home to the "Power Breakfast" and executive lunches. It features contemporary cuisine in a warm and inviting setting.

In the evening 540 Park is magically transformed into Feinstein's at The Regency. Having made its debut on October 1999, it has become known as "The Nightclub of New York" showcasing such great talents as Michael Feinstein (the club's namesake), Linda Eder, Rosemary Clooney, John Pizzarrelli and Ronan Tynan.

The Library, located next to 540 Park, offers the style and comfort of a residential lounge, perfect for meeting friends or conducting informal business. It offers early morning breakfast to late night cocktails in a warm and intimate setting.

The Grand Suite

John Iachetti, Executive Chef, plans the menus for all of the hotels' dining venues changing them seasonally.

Casa at The Regency is complimentary to all guests and is managed by Casa Private Fitness, one of the best health and fitness clubs in the country. It features state of the art equipment to meet a guests exercise needs. Additional services such as one-on-one training are available for a fee.

The Regency Hotel is also child and pet friendly offering special amenities and services for these special guests. Also in-house is a concierge; Nico Salon, a full service salon, and an on-site limousine service.

540 park

The Library

Feinstein's at The Regency

The Lucerne

NEW YORK

The Lucerne is one of New York's most treasured landmarks. Elegantly restored into a luxury boutique hotel, it has been rated as the #1 hotel in New York City with special recognition for service and value. The Lucerne is located on the lovely upper West Side amidst a friendly brownstone-filled neighborhood, with many boutique shops and charming cafes. The Lucerne is only a short walk to Central Park and the Museum of Natural History. It is also minutes away from Lincoln Center, Broadway and Times Square.

Hotel amenities include an 880 sq. ft. penthouse meeting space with an outside patio overlooking the Hudson River and Manhattan, complimentary continental breakfast, fitness center, business center, in-room movies, internet T.V., nintendo game system, PC link, full size iron and ironing board, coffee maker and complimentary coffee, hair dryer, marble bathrooms, choice of complimentary newspapers, and individually climate controlled rooms and suites. Dry cleaning services are also available.

From the magnificently adorned exterior, to the warmth and graciousness of our staff, you are invited to enjoy an unparalleled level of luxury and hospitality that will surely surpass your highest expectations.

Lucerne Suite

201 THE LUCERNE

The Lucerne

A Stylish Private retreat for

The Franklin Hotel is located on a quiet side street adjacent to the restaurant and entertainment quarter of the Upper East Side. A stylish, private retreat within a short walk of Manhattan's best museums, auction houses, restaurants and boutiques.

Illuminated beds with billowing white canopies, custom designed Sherwood and steel furnishings together with exceptional art and fresh flowers impart a wonderfully romantic and mysterious aura to the hotel's forty-eight guestrooms.

he discriminating travellers

Complimentary amenities include Continental European Breakfast, shoe shine, bottled spring water, VCR televisions with American and Foreign film library, cedar closets, hand held showers, oversized Irish cotton towels and Neutrogena bath accompaniment

With The Franklin Hotel every guest will experience warm and friendly smiles, excellent service and comfort making your visit to New York a memorable one.

Spacious and comfortable guest room

Welcome to the Hotel Wales, a Madison Avenue landmark which has been lovingly restored to its original turn-of-the century charm. The serene atmosphere and intimate scale of the hotel are immediately felt upon entering the lobby and has been carefully carried throughout, making each room a comfortable retreat. Each morning, the Hotel Wales greets you with the delightful complimentary European breakfast served in the enchanting Pied Piper Room. The fitness center allows you to gear up for the day or unwind after your day is complete. Throughout your stay, Hotel Wales wants you to savor the civilized

Al fresco penthouse patio

New York of a bygone era. With personalized service, the Hotel Wales' gracious staff strives to make each guest feel at home.

Hotel Wales exudes a contemporary view of New York charm. Quietly grand, yet forever alive with motion. European in style, American in comfort, this landmark hotel envelops you in rich jewel tones, carved woods, tapestries and oriental rugs. In true Upper Eastside style, it is intimate, inviting, irresistibly posh. Experience the Hotel Wales, the place to visit Old New York today.

THE EXCELSIOR
H O T E L

Excelsior Lobby

The Excelsior Hotel is a luxurious establishment offering elegance, class and a caring staff. Located between Central Park West and post Columbus Avenue, it overlooks the beautiful park-like atmosphere of the American Museum of Natural History and the Rose Center for Earth & Space.

Having undergone a complete renovation, the Excelsior Hotel features 116 newly renovated guest rooms and 80 enchanting suites adorned in a French country motif. Impressive balconies also accentuate some rooms. Conveniently added to the rooms are two line telephones with data-port, voice-mail messaging and inroom fax machines. All rooms feature remote control television with lodgenet, on demand movies and Nintendo for those guests who want a pleasant at-home stay. Other facilities that add to the appeal of the hotel include same day valet laundry service, overnight shoeshine service and express checkouts. A cozy entertainment room

is available to clients who may want to relax from a busy day at work or sightseeing. This charming room consists of a library, fitness center and conference room, and surround-sound state of the art video/television. While roaming the outside of the Excelsior, guests will find two enclosed terraces, which are peaceful enough to read a good book or have a cool refreshment during the warm summer months.

The neighborhood surrounding this four star hotel features families, craft markets and the opportunity to take a stroll in Central Park. For those particular guests who desire more than just a ``tourist'' hotel, the Excelsior is the perfect place to situate. The area swells with "Old World New York Charm" offering an endless range of restaurants, exclusive shops and outdoor cafes when in season. The attractive surrounding of the hotel include historic apartment buildings and brownstones along with tree-lined streets and turn of the century lampposts. It provides an early

twentieth century feel to guests who hunger for the class and exquisiteness of uptown New York.

While lodging in the Excelsior, guests have the opportunity to frequent popular New York visitor sites. The hotel is just a walk away fromthe Beacon and Lincoln theatres. Not too far away on the East side of Central park is the Metropolitan Museum of Art, the Guggenheim, the Whitney and boutiques on Madison Avenue. Other favorite sites to visit that are close to the Excelsior are Columbia University and the Cathedral of St. John the Divine. For those who enjoy the hustle and bustle of the city, nearby public transportation will be able to take guests to Times Square in just a matter of minutes.

The Excelsior Hotel is the perfect place to stay if you desire a taste of grace, distinction, and superior service in a trendy town. The fashionable rooms and elegant surroundings have made the Excelsior a delightful spot for guests to enjoy.

Excelsior Dining Room

Excelsior Hotel features enchanting rooms adorned in a French country motif

Holiday Inn

Wall Street District

Hotel Room

The first newly built hotel in 10 years, situated in the heart of the Financial and Technology districts, The Holiday Inn Wall Street offers deluxe hotel services and amenities with a flair towards serving the needs of the Hi-Tech Executive. This hotel is nothing like your parents' "green sign" Holiday Inn and while relatively new, it is already a favorite of those visiting downtown Manhattan.

New York City's most technologically advanced hotel, each room features computers with Micro Soft Office Applications, DVD/CD players and secure network printers as well as T1 Internet Connectivity. It also provides cellular connect services, transferring calls made to your guestroom to your cellular phone, direct dial guest room phone numbers as well as portable phones. Guestrooms are virtual offices equipped with six-foot work desks, free office supplies, voicemail, data ports, safes, mini bars,

and ergonomic furniture. Marble bathrooms with lighted makeup mirrors; rainforest showerheads, English amenities, terry bath sheets and robes.

Also a first for Manhattan, S.M.A.R.T. rooms offer wireless internet ready laptop computers (for use in and out of the hotel), printers, complimentary breakfast and cocktail service as well as upgraded amenities and services.

The hotel also offers a complete Business Center with computers, laptop docking stations, fax and copy machines, and is open 24 hours, as is the hotels' virtual gift shop as well as room service from a real New York Deli. Exercise facilities are available both on and off property with equipment deliverable to your guestroom as well.

The Platinum Café offers Italian cuisine in a casual atmosphere and features an Express Breakfast Buffet, to start your day off right, and a Happy Hour exclusively for hotel guests. Beyond Room Service allows you to sample cuisines from seven local ethnic restaurants which (opened in June 1999) can be delivered to your room.

A Hi- Tech boardroom with seating for up to 50 people comes fully equipped with audio visual equipment including T1 access and power point presentation capabilities.

The hotel is also within minutes of famous downtown landmarks such as the World Trade Center, the Statue Of Liberty, and South Street Seaport as well as the dynamic neighborhoods of Chelsea, Tribecca, Soho, Little Italy and China Town.

Perfect for business or leisure, the hotel is the easiest decision on Wall Street.

Holiday Inn Lobby

*Platinum Café offers Italian
cuisine in a casual atmosphere*

the NEW YORKER
RAMADA
HOTEL

A good view of the expansive lobby

The New Yorker Ramada, located on the corner of Eighth Avenue and 34th Street, is at the very heart of the Big Apple. A living landmark, the hotel features a magnificent, trend-setting Art Deco design. Its brilliant architecture, interesting history and comfortable accommodations make the New Yorker Ramada a top choice for city visitors.

The hotel opened on January 4, 1930 as New York's largest hotel. It then prospered in the 1930s and 40s during the Swing and Big Band eras, drawing in not only business visitors and tourists but the society elite. Business declined in subsequent years, however, and in 1972 the New Yorker closed as a hotel. It was purchased twice afterwards, with plans to convert it to a medical school and then as a headquarters for church missionaries. Then, in 1994, the building reopened as a hotel, once again restoring its reputation as one of New York's classiest hotels.

Having undergone recent renovations, the New Yorker Ramada features 1,000 newly decorated, stylish guest-rooms and suites. Each window has its own panoramic view, so guests can enjoy the city from the comfort of their rooms. Visitors can also appreciate a number of hotel amenities, including Cable and Pay-Per-View

Conference room a boon to the business executives or meeting planners

movies, data port adaptable telephones, individually controlled air conditioning and heating, a multilingual staff and 24-hour security. A state-of the-art Fitness Center and Personal Business Center are located in the lower lobby for convenience. In addition, guests can enjoy the newly renovated, 5,000 square feet hotel lobby, which is also decorated in a trendy, art deco style.

To satisfy visitors' appetites, the hotel also includes La Vigna Ristorante and Bar, which features delicious Italian and Continental cuisine in a cozy, intimate setting. Guests can also grab a bite to eat at the Tick Tock Diner, a 50s-style eatery open twenty-four hours. In addition to the diner, the Lobby Café, located next to the concierge desk, serves cappuccino, espresso and pastries.

The New Yorker Ramada is perfectly situated, located just one block from Madison Square Garden and Macy's, and only three blocks to the Empire State Building and Fifth Avenue. It is conveniently adjacent to the Pennsylvania Railroad Station and is the closest hotel to the Javits Convention Center. In addition, the hotel is a five-minute walk to Times Square and has direct access to public transportation. Indeed, whether it be for business, sight-seeing, or shopping The New Yorker Ramada is the perfect place to stay- "If you're not in New Yorker Ramada you're not in New York."

Lobby topped with 15-foot vaulted ceiling

the MuSe

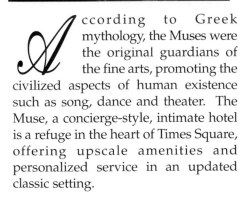

*A*ccording to Greek mythology, the Muses were the original guardians of the fine arts, promoting the civilized aspects of human existence such as song, dance and theater. The Muse, a concierge-style, intimate hotel is a refuge in the heart of Times Square, offering upscale amenities and personalized service in an updated classic setting.

The Muse has been designed to have a contemporary feel, drawing upon influences of historic New York hotels, with references to the proportion and symmetry of classic architecture. Entering the hotel from 46th Street, guests arrive in a lobby topped with a 15-foot vaulted ceiling. Custom-patterned, marble-and-granite flooring covers the unobstructed expanse of the lobby, while wool carpet runners by Edward Field define the

seating areas flanking either side. The residential feel of the lobby is emphasized through updated custom furnishings like overstuffed sofas, rolled-arm lounge chairs and oversized lamps in a soft, warm palette of plum, burgundy, rust and pale blue-green, with touches of iridescence throughout.

Travelers familiar with the often cramped quarters available at New York hotels will be pleasantly surprised by the spaciousness of The Muse's guest rooms and baths. In-room amenities include: cable television with HBO and Time-Warner movies on demand; Sony alarm clock with CD player; high-speed Internet access; multi-line cordless phone with dataport and voicemail; Direct Inward Dialing private line; refreshment center; personal safe; European bed linens, featherbeds and duvets; European cotton bathrobe and cotton towels; toiletries by Philosophy; hairdryer; iron and ironing board; coffee maker and complimentary newspaper. Guest services includes twice-daily maid service, in house spa services, a fitness center and valet parking.

The emphasis at The Muse is anticipatory service, with each and every guest treated as a VIP by the hotel's concierge staff. The Muse's sit-down reception desk emphasizes the personal attention and service offered to its guests from check-in to check-out. Weary travelers can also by-pass the reception desk and be escorted immediately to their rooms by a concierge manager. The hotel's innovative "Midnight Pantry" will offer guests the luxury of raiding a complimentary buffet of freshly baked cookies and desserts, fresh fruit-plates after an evening of theater, or before turning in for the night, according to Mark Briskin, The Muse's General Manager.

The Muse's three meeting areas can provide the ideal setting for business meetings and special events. The hotel offers two director-level board rooms, offering seating for 8 to 10 people each, and a 930 square-foot, multi-purpose function room that can be used to accommodate up to 80 people.

Just steps from the lights of Broadway, The Muse aspires to re-define contemporary convenience and comfort.

ON THE AVE
HOTEL

View of Manhattan Skyline

*L*ike the famed restaurants and shops that distinguish the Upper West Side, ON THE AVE personifies its neighborhood.

Its very essence is rich with the Manhattan qualities that New Yorkers experience every day of their lives - and with the service and features expected of a leading hotel.

Perfect complement to tempo of the Upper West Side, ON THE AVE's accommodations include Penthouse, King and Queen rooms. A state of the art communication and entertainment system connects guests to hotel services, the Internet, shopping, sports, transportation and, of course, the world's greatest city.

Meticulous created rooms present striking furnishings in an environment rich with texture and light. These features are well defined from the innovative lobby to the distinctive guest rooms.

ON THE AVE has redefined the hotel stay in New York. Stainless steel fixtures in the remarkable baths accent the exceptional design of what is sure to be considered one of the outstanding hotels of its time.

Just a short walk to major international attractions such as the American Museum of Natural History and Central Park — and New York highlights like Zabar's and Cafe Des Artistes — ON THE AVE delivers the ultimate New York experience.

Rooms are carefully designed for comfort and convenience

Views from the Penthouse are as dramatic as the rooms themselves.

The Sheraton Experience: Accommodating, Innovative, Liberating, Worldly And Respectful.

An inviting oasis from the bustling world outside, the **Sheraton JFK Airport Hotel** offers the added convenience of being located just one mile from the JFK International Airport terminals. Newly renovated and furnished in a European décor, this well-appointed hotel provides guests everything they need for a seamless meeting experience including the finest in service and hospitality, thanks to a responsive and caring staff. All accommodations at the Sheraton JFK Airport Hotel feature welcome comforts, including a hair dryer and makeup mirror in the bathroom. Each room is also equipped with essential office features such as dual phone lines and dataport, and voicemail. Unwinding after work is equally effortless, thanks to the hotel's fitness room and distinctive dining.

When it's time for business, the hotel's 3,800 square feet of meeting and banquet space offers a wide variety of planning options. The facilities feature state-of-the-art audiovisual equipment, and each event is overseen by an attentive, dedicated staff ensuring you have just the meeting experience you expect.

Sheraton
HOTELS & RESORTS
Sheraton JFK Airport Hotel
151-20 Baisley Blvd., Jamaica Queens, NY 11434
(718) 489-1000 • Fax (718) 489-1002

GRAND LUXURY
IN THE HEART OF THE AIRPORT

Accommodations/Special Events

At the Crowne Plaza LaGuardia, we accommodate guests in comfort and style. Designed with both business and leisure travelers in mind, each of our 358 deluxe guest rooms creates a pleasurable environment for work and relaxation. All of our guests enjoy the luxury of two phones with voice mail, computer data ports, coffee maker, irons and ironing boards, extra large desk and hair dryers. 158 spacious Business Traveler rooms, each with queen bed, refrigerator, extra large bathrooms and ample work space to pamper the executive traveler.

Hospitality Suites are the perfect setting for VIP meetings or celebrations. Complete indoor Health Club facilities, indoor pool, whirlpool, sauna, state of the art exercise.

Executive Level features luxurious guest rooms, American breakfast and evening hors d'oeuvres served with compliments in the private lounge, complimentary newspaper and nightly turndown service. And, of course, a professional concierge will assist your special travel and entertainment needs.

Pavilion Restaurant an enticing array of culinary delights and is ideal for business and social gatherings. For guests that prefer privacy, guest room dining is available from 6:00 AM to 12:00 Midnight.

Embers Lounge unwind in front of one of the fireplaces while enjoying generous sumptuous complimentary social hour hors-d'oeuvres.

Conference Center featuring 12,500 Sq. ft. of meeting space, teleconferencing capabilities, computer hook-ups, a sophisticated in-house audiovisual department and a professional meeting staff experienced in creating successful events.

An exclusive multi-tiered theater, with classroom seating for up to 60 with internet access at each seat, highlights the 15 versatile banquet and conference rooms which includes a private board room seating 12.

A Symphony of Taste

Milk-Chocolate/ hazlenut tart with mango/ black-tea-infused whipped cream, by Remy Funfrock
Photo by: *John Uher*

Chef Daniel Boulud
***Photo by:** Peter Medilek*

DANIEL

Considered one of the world's leading chefs Daniel Boulud is known for the exquisite cuisine he serves. Born in France Daniel was raised on his family's farm near Lyon, where he grew up surrounded by the rhythms of the seasons, the wonders of produce fresh from the fields, and of course, his grandmother's inspiring home cooking.

After being nominated as candidate for best cooking apprentice in France, Daniel went on to train under some of the country's most renowned Chefs such as Roger Vergé, Georges Blanc and Michel Guérard. Following two years as Chef in some of Copenhagen's finest kitchens, Daniel made his way to the United States where his first position was as Chef to The European Commission in Washington, DC. Next, Daniel went on to open the Polo Lounge at he Westbury Hotel and later Le Régence at the Hotel Plaza Athenée in New York City. From 1986 to 1992, Daniel served as Executive Chef at New York's Le Cirque. During his tenure there, the restaurant was regularly chosen as one of the most highly rated in the country.

In 1993, Daniel Boulud opened his own much-heralded restaurant DANIEL on Manhattan's Upper East Side. Here his inspiration remained the seasonal ingredients drawn from the best local purveyors. In just a year after opening, the restaurant was rated "one of the ten best restaurants in the world".

In September 1998 Daniel Boulud opened Café Boulud, named for the gathering place his great grandparents tended on their farm outside Lyon at the turn of the century. The contemporary Café Boulud is a French restaurant with an international accent welcoming Manhattan's cafe society to a spot with the cosmopolitan chic of a Parisian rendez-vous. In December of the same year the chef-restaurateur relocated DANIEL to its new Venetian renaissance inspired setting in the former Mayfair Hotel on Park Avenue and 65th Street. Since the restaurant's re-opening Daniel Boulud has been named "Chef of the year" by Bon Appétit Magazine and has received Gourmet magazine's "Top Table" award as well as four stars from the New York Times.

Daniel's classic Renaissance-style Dining Room
Photo by: *Sinichiro Inoue*

A cadre of more than 40 meticulously trained cooks prepare the Chef's seasonal cuisine inspired by the market in 4000 square feet of state-of-the-art-kitchens. At his new restaurant, Daniel Boulud and his staff strive to offer the elegant ambiance, gracious service, delectable foods and wines that epitomize "la grande restauration Francaise" in the heart of Manhattan's Upper East Side.

Interior designer Patrick Naggar and architect Frank Williams have taken the former Mayfair Hotel lobby and combined it with the old Le Cirque restaurant returning them to their original 1920's Renaissance-inspired splendor. Each room is accented with beautifully restored neo-classical details such as carved pilasters, balustrades and limestone finishes. Bronze-studded mahogany doors guide the eye toward 18-foot coffered and stenciled ceilings offset by mahogany beams. Each room is suffused with a warm bouquet of burgundy, pale rose and soft yellow hues adorning Patrick Naggar's custom furnishings and richly textured fabrics.

Daniel Boulud is delighted to offer his clients The Bellecour room (named for a square in the heart of his hometown of Lyon), an elegant private function room for festive entertaining. The Bellecour Room seats up to 80 guests for lunch and dinner and is a perfect setting for both private and corporate celebrations. The banquet chef and manager will take personal care of every detail of our your entertaining needs.

The cuisine at Daniel celebrates nature's bounty, taking each season's most glorious ingredients and revealing their delicious flavors. Daniel Boulud starts with respect for french culinary tradition and reinterprets it for the contemporary palate. At Daniel, you may expect to find a time honored Poulet Roti en Croute de Sel prepared according to the most respected technique, or you may encounter classics "with a twist" that Daniel has re-invented in his own whimsical fashion. It is this combination of the classical and the contemporary that keeps guests intrigued and delighted.

At press time, the Chef was in the midst of opening "DB ", his new casual bistro in the City Club Hotel on West 44th Street. "DB " is an easy going and contemporary dining spot in the heart of midtown and just steps from the theater district. Here Daniel Boulud's latest menu offers updated bistro cooking rooted in French tradition and occasionally accented with global flavors.

Luxury Bar and Lounge at Daniel
***Photo by:** Sinichiro Inoue*

Maine Peeky Toe Crab Salad in a Green Apple Gelée
Photo by: *Bruno Hausch*

Chilled Tomato Soup with Eggplant Compote
Photo by: *Philippe Houzé*

Braised Lamb Shank with Asparagus & Porcini
Photo by: *Philippe Houzé*

CAFÉ BOULUD

Café Boulud's menu pays homage to the food Daniel grew up with in France and celebrates the food he loves in America. At Café Boulud, Daniel and executive Chef, Andrew Carmellini, offer their favorite dishes drawn from family recipes, regional specialties and haute cuisine. The menu is presented under the headings of Daniel's four culinary muses. Guests are encouraged to sample courses from as many of these mini-menus as they wish. The menu's four headings are:

"La Tradition", the classic dishes of French cooking. These are the dishes Daniel grew up with, the family meals his mother and grandmother prepared, the food of the original turn of the century Café Boulud tended by his great grandparents and the first recipes he prepared as an apprentice in Lyon. But the classics are neither historical nor immutable for Daniel. He uses ingredients different from those of the originals, and serves them to people with disparate tastes, diets and culinary affections. Daniel prepares dishes such as a pot-au-feu or bouillabaisse with American ingredients, updated to delight a new, young audience and to rekindle fond taste memories in those who knew them years ago.

"La Saison", the seasonal specialties of the market. The family farm in the Lyon countryside where Daniel grew up produced a wide variety of seasonal crops in its fields, orchards and vegetable gardens. Farm animals included cows for milk, goats for cheese, and pigs for charcuterie, while the farmyard was resplendent with geese, ducks, chickens, squabs, rabbits, guinea fowls, and turkeys. Each new crop was celebrated with festive meals. Since cooking in the United States, Daniel has established close relationships with the country's most passionate farmers and dedicated purveyors whose wonderful products inspire his dishes. Here at Café Boulud, the menu showcases the delicacies of each season's bounty. From foraged mushrooms, diver scallops with roe, hand-picked berries, wild grouse, line-caught halibut, to jumbo white asparagus, our clientele will savor the season's best ingredients.

"Le Potager", a celebration of the vegetable garden. Daniel's favorite spot on the farm was the vegetable garden where his parents grew the organic produce, herbs and flowers they sold at the Lyon farmer's market. Preparing each vegetable while respecting its flavor had been Daniel's favorite challenge as a Chef. At Café Boulud, the dishes of Le Potager are completely vegetarian and, in most cases, very low in fat. Some of Daniel's signature soups, Chilled Five Spring Pea Soup, Chilled Tomato Soup with a Basil Guacamole, Swiss Chard and Bean Soup with Ricotta Toasts and the Curried Cream of Cauliflower and Apple Soup provide for light and flavorful appetizers along with vibrant salads. Entrees include fricassées of seasonal vegetables, vegetable risottos, raviolis and pastas. Wild mushrooms and truffles are celebrated along with baby beets, jumbo sweet garlic, caramelized turnips and roasted endive.

"Le Voyage", the travels that have introduced Daniel to the exotic flavors of world cuisines. Forever curious about other cultures and traditions, Daniel constantly searches for new ingredients, flavors, and recipes to add to his repertoire. Just as he does with foods from La Tradition, Daniel passes the dishes of a region through his own culinary filters. Working with world renowned visiting chefs from other countries, as well as with his own team of cooks (a veritable global village), Daniel creates dishes that, while celebrating the roots, spirit and fundamental flavors of a particular place, will also sing out with his signature style. To launch Café Boulud, Le Voydge dishes featured Spanish and Basque specialties.

On the **dessert menu**, Daniel and Pastry Chef, Rémy Fünfrock, work together to create dishes in harmony with the savory menu's four muses. Traditional selections re-visited from a contemporary point of view might include classic favorites such as a tart tatin or île flottante. Seasonal desserts focus on lighter offerings inspired by the bounty of the orchard, such as fragrant sorbets, poached fruits and fruit tarts. Finally, desserts from "Le Voyage" are accentuated with the exotic spices and ingredients that flavor the world's sweets.

Terrace
Photo by: *Patrick Rytikangas*

Interior
Photo by: *Patrick Rytikangas*

Lemon-Lime Asparagus Risotto
Photo by: *Gentl & Hyers*

Chicken Grande Mére Francine
Photo by: *Gentl & Hyers*

121

Zucchini and Ricotta with Tomato Confit
Photo by: *Gentl & Hyers*

Rhubarb and Orange-Flower Millefeuille
Photo by: *Gentl & Hyers*

OCEANA
RESTAURANT

The extraordinary legacy of the Livanos Family, John, wife Chrysa, and children Nick, Bill and Corina, in the New York restaurant industry began more than forty years ago when John Livanos immigrated to the U. S. from Greece.

At Oceana, an international approach to seafood is the foundation. Classical cooking techniques anchor Oceana's cuisine, which springs from executive chef/partner Rick Moonen's vivid taste memories, global travels and keen, yet playful imagination. Recipes are inventive yet familiar, striking the perfect balance between flavor and seasoning.

The menu is based on seasonally available seafood and shellfish, augmented by the global pantry. Appetizers include: signature Jumbo Lump Crab Cake with Chipotle Pepper Sauce and Carrot Salad with Nuoc Cham; Wild Striped Bass Ceviche with Grapefruit, Lemon Verbena, Jalapeno Peppers and Grilled Flatbread; Yellowfin Tuna Tartar with Yuzu Wasabi Vinaigrette; Sesame Seaweed Salad, and Rick Moonen's Onion Cured Gravlax with Sweet Pepper Relish, Black Bean Cakes and Cilantro Cream, as well as a true Caesar Salad with Fresh White Anchovies and Garlic Croutons. Main courses: Grilled Striped Bass with Beefsteak Tomato Tart, Calamata Olives, Caramelized Onions and Red Wine Reduction; Butter Poached Lobster with Asparagus Flan, Foraged Mushrooms, Potato Crisp and Black Truffle Vinaigrette; Grilled Diver Sea Scallops with Horseradish Mashed Potatoes, Braised Oxtail and Caramelized Root Vegetables; "Everything" Crusted Tuna Steak (like the bagel), served with Caponata and Grain Salad, Roasted Red Pepper Coulis and Cucumber Yogurt Drizzle; Grilled Dourade Royale with Braised Artichokes, Fennel & Parisian Potatoes and Herbed Riesling Broth.

David Carmichael has won critical acclaim for his hallmark confections, and is responsible for preparing all breads and desserts, including daily selections of freshly made ice creams and sorbets. The menu changes constantly with the seasons. Signature desserts include: Chocolate Hazelnut Mousse Cake with Coconut Sorbet; Pistachio Bombe with Chocolate Chip Chiffon Cake and Pistachio Meringue; Creme Brulee served with Huckleberry Syrup and Dulce de Leche; Key Lime Pie with Graham Cracker Crust and Orange Segments; English Blue Stilton & Shropshire Blue Cheese served with Lingonberry Poached Pear, Ruby Port Sauce and Pastry Chef Sampler combinations which include: Sticky Toffee Pudding, Pistachio Bombe, Chocolate Gratin, Key Lime Pie & Apple Sorbet or Chestnut Baked Alaska, Apple Crumb Cake, Creme Brulee and Banana Strudel & Raspberry Sorbet.

The decor and dining areas of Oceana consist of: the first floor dining room featuring intimate tables and plush banquettes with seating for 60 guests. Two private dining rooms — the "Salon" upstairs doubles as a dining room during regular service. Without banquettes, the seating for 60 is flexible. The very private wine cellar below street level, accommodates 24.

The second floor lounge benefits from dramatic ceiling height and floor to ceiling wine storage. Situated under the watchful eye of the restaurant's show piece, an elegant copper grouper, the bar offers stools, banquettes and cocktail tables. Bar dining is encouraged: a separate bar menu features fresh shucked oysters and crispy calamari, as well as any regular menu item. Cigar and cigarette smoking is permitted upstairs in the lounge.

Dark woods, leather seating, well-placed posters and clever lighting are handsome yet comfortable. Unique is the "wine cellar," where elegant table settings, terra cotta tile and wine racks create the feeling of dining in a French cave. The service is always accommodating and professional.

Private parties and catering fall under the direction of owner Corina Livanos. Menus and service are tailored to each event. Two private dining rooms allow flexibility in accommodations.

Under the careful attention of wine director Doug Bernthal and managing partner Paul McLaughlin, the Oceana wine list now includes more white varietals, greater depth in Italian wines and vertical tastings of some of the most prized reds produced in Bordeaux and California

The wine list, with 1,000 selections, is deep in white wines (with an extensive roster of fruity, acidic, Rieslings) & seafood-friendly reds such as Pinot Noir, Syrah and Cabernet Franc. Depth in vintages can be seen in the collection of 185 white Burgundies and serious west coast Chardonnay. Champagne, sparkling and dessert wines, premium beer, cognac and brandy, plus single malts, and small batch bourbons.

"Everthing" Crusted Tuna Steak
Caponata and Grain Salad, Roasted Red Pepper Coulis
Cucumber Yogurt Drizzle

Moroccan Spiced Salmon
Served on a bed of Lentils & Red Pepper Coulis

Sticky Toffee Pudding
Banana Cashew Ice Cream

Cosmopolitan Shopping Pleasures

Bergdorf Goodman Counter

Bergdorf Goodman

Exterior of Bergdorf Goodman

As the leading fashion specialty store, Bergdorf Goodman is recognized throughout the world for its elegant, luxe environment, quality customer service and keen eye on style. Located at Fifth Avenue and 58th Street, perhaps the world's most preeminent retail location, it is much a part of New York as Central Park or the Metropolitan Museum of Art.

Bergdorf Goodman, as it is known today, had its start in 1899 when a young Edwin Goodman moved to Manhattan and began working for the master tailor Herman Bergdorf in his store on Fifth Avenue and 19th Street.

The two men created stylish clothing for distinguished women and in 1901 formed the Bergdorf Goodman partnership. Together they opened a larger store on 32nd Street and their salon resembled a great Parisian couture house. Edwin Goodman eventually bought out the elder Herman Bergdorf, but kept the store's name intact.

In 1914, Edwin Goodman relocated the establishment to larger quarters on Fifth Avenue where Rockefeller Center now stands. It was in this location that Goodman became the first couturier to sell elegant, ready-made fashions from the best American and French manufacturers, thereby eliminating the long, tedious fittings required for tailored couture clothing.

In 1928 Bergdorf Goodman moved into its present structure, a newly constructed building at Fifth Avenue and 58th Street, on the former site of the great Cornelious Vanderbilt mansion. Andrew Goodman, son of Edwin, took over the store's operation in 1953. In 1972 he sold Bergdorf Goodman to Carter Hawley Hale Stores and shortly thereafter retired his position in 1975.

Goodman passed away in 1993. Ira Neimark joined the organization as President in 1975 and immediately initiated a $15 million store renovation. Simultaneously Stephen Elkin joined Bergdorf Goodman as senior vice president and chief financial officer in 1978 and in 1980 he was named executive vice president of finance and operations. Mr. Elkin became vice chairman and chief operating officer in 1985.

Bergdorf Goodman emerged as a leader in discovering and recognizing European and American talent with many famed European designers making early debuts at the store. Exclusivity and collection launches are synonymous with Bergdorfs. Over the next several years, many refinements and additions were made to the store including the redesign of the First floor and a fine accessories court featuring exclusive boutiques. In 1986, "The Decorative Home on Seven" was created. Bergdorf Goodman Men, the

Bergdorf Goodman Counter

ultimate store for gentlemen," opened its doors in 1990, directly across the street at 745 Fifth Avenue and is recognized as an elegant yet accessible shopping environment unlike any other.

In 1987, The Neiman Marcus Group acquired Bergdorf Goodman. Today, the Neiman Marcus Group is a sixty-percent owned subsidiary of its publicly owned parent company, Harcourt General Corporation. In December 1990, accomplished merchant Burton Tansky joined the store as vice chairman and Mr. Elkin was appointed President retaining his chief operating officer responsibilities. In February 1992, Tansky was named chairman and chief executive officer.

1992 marked the dramatic change in spirit and atmosphere for Bergdorf's Fifth Floor. Formerly the Miss Bergdorf department, it was redesigned and named "On 5ive." This vibrant, contemporary atmosphere featured a large accessories area, shoe department and "Café on 5ive,"

a restaurant reflects its stylish surroundings.

Effective May 1994, changes in the executive structure of the Neiman Marcus Group were announced. Burton Tansky was appointed chairman and chief executive officer of Neiman Marcus Stores and Stephen Elkin; formerly president and chief operating officer of Bergdorf Goodman was named Mr. Tansky's successor as chairman and chief executive officer. Dawn Mello returned to Bergdorf Goodman as President, a post she previously held from 1983 to 1989.

The John Barrett Salon and the Susan Cimminelli Spa opened in June 1997 in the penthouse apartment,which formerly housed the residence of the Goodman family. In the summer of 1999, Dawn Mello, resigned her position as President of the store. Bergdorf Goodman hired veteran retailer executive, Peter Rizzo as Vice Chairman in April 1999, and later promoted him to President in

September of 1999. In the fall of 1998, Bergdorf Goodman announced plans to more than double the size of its cosmetics area to 15,000 square feet. In November 1999 "The New Level of Beauty" opened.

In April 2000, Ronald L. Frasch was named chairman and chief executive officer of Bergdorf Goodman. Frasch joined the store from GFT USA where he was President for four years. Prior to that he was President and chief executive officer of Escada USA from 1994 to 1996. From 1984 to 1994 Mr. Frasch was Senior Vice President and General Merchandise Manager for Women's Apparel at Neiman Marcus Stores. Earlier he was Division Merchandise Manager and Store Manager at Saks. He began his retailing career at Bloomingdales.

On April 17, 1872, brothers Lyman and Joseph opened a humble store on Third Avenue called the "Great East Side Bazaar". Who would have guessed this shop, which specialized in selling skirts, corsets, hosiery, millinery and gloves, would be the beginning of what ultimately grew into one of the most well-known and exclusive chains of department stores: Bloomingdale's. Today, the flagship store is located on the posh Upper East Side of Manhattan, just three blocks from the original shop. But this area was not always the home of the well-to-do. When the Bloomingdale brothers were looking for a site for their new store the heart of New York's shopping district was Union Square. Stores like F.A.O. Schwarz, Gorman and Company and W & J Sloan were all located in the area of 14th Street and Fifth Avenue, as were most of their customers.

However, the visionary brothers sensed the Upper East Side's potential. The city had recently purchased a huge area of land and was creating the urban haven that is now called Central Park. In addition, the Metropolitan Museum of Art had just opened on Fifth Avenue and 53rd Street. The brothers were confident that these attractions would draw visitors, so in 1872 they risked everything and opened the shop against the advice of many.

The gamble paid off. Within a few years, the brothers business was so successful – offering the latest styles including hoop skirts – that they needed a larger space. In 1880 they expanded into a five-story building on the corner of 56th Street and Third Avenue. On October 5, 1886, the operation moved to its current site on Third Avenue and 59th Street. The six story store was state-of-the-art. It was the first to include theatre-like windows for browsing and passenger elevators. By 1929, Bloomingdale's covered an entire city block. And in 1931, the Art Deco edifice by architects Starret and Van Vleck was completed.

Over the next several decades the leaders of Bloomingdale's continued running the business in the same entrepreneurial manner as its founders did. In 1980 Bloomingdale's set another precedent. Entering into virtually uncharted territory, store representatives visited areas of the People's Republic of China that had been closed to foreigners for thirty years. Today buyers continue to travel the globe to find exclusive items. They also continue to lure new designers, just as they once managed to convince Yves St. Laurent, Calvin Klein, Claude Montana and Thierry Mulger to open their first in-store boutiques. Bloomingdale's also differentiates itself from competitors by focusing on customer service and offering special events like personal appearances and fashion shows.

Now a division of Federated Department Stores, Inc., in 1996 the chain became national opening five new locations in California. There are currently 23 stores in the United States.

Barneys New York

$\mathcal{B}$arneys New York was founded in 1923 by Barney Pressman who pawned his wife's engagement ring at her suggestion to raise the $500 to cover the rent and to stock forty suits.

In its early years, Barneys New York built its business by offering quality clothing at discount prices while providing the attention to detail and service that remain the stores' hallmark. Under Barney Pressman's leadership, the small storefront shop grew in both size and selection.

In the late 60's, Fred Pressman, Barney's son and his family began to transform Barneys New York from a discount retailer to a specialty retailer. In addition to clothing and accessories, the store grew to include a restaurant and Chelsea Passage. This unique gift and antique shop offers exclusive collections of china, glass, silver as well as antique jewelry.

In the late 70's, Barneys New York became the first Men's Store to feature European designers and assembled the most complete selection of designer Men's fashion. In 1976, the designs of Giorgio Armani were introduced to America demonstrating its on-going commitment to discovering and developing new and innovative design

talent. In the same year it brought Armani to America, Barneys New York added a women's department to what had become the largest men's clothing store in the world.

In the late 80's, the Pressman family formed a new retail company that operates stores across the country under the Barneys New York name. The stores feature well-priced fashion and designer merchandise for men and women in a setting, which reflects the high quality and service levels that Barneys New York is known for.

Also in the same year Barneys New York announced an exclusive joint venture agreement with Isetan Company Limited, one of Japan's largest retailers. The first Barneys New York store in Japan opened in the Shinjuku section of Tokyo in November 1990. At 40,000-square feet, it is the largest freestanding specialty store in Japan associated with an American retailer. Barneys New York opened its second store in Japan, August 1993 in Yokohama.

In the Fall of 1993, Barneys New York opened a 230,000-square foot store at Madison Avenue and 61st Street. It continues to be the largest specialty store built in Manhattan in more than sixty years. Approximately

half of the store is devoted to menswear, the balance is women's clothing, accessories, and Chelsea Passage.

Barneys New York also opened Beverly Hills with a merchandise mix similar to Madison Avenue. This 110,000-square foot store is located on Wilshire Drive just one block west of Rodeo Drive.

In an ironic twist of fate, Barneys New York re-established a presence in the retail discount business in 1993. In that year the first outlet store at Woodbury Common in Harriman, New York was opened. Its success precipitated the opening of twelve additional outlets.

The traditional Warehouse Sale in Manhattan (inaugurated in 1970) began to travel in 1995. In addition to New York City, Barneys New York currently operated Warehouse Sales in Beverly Hills and Chicago. In May of 2000, the first freestanding CO-OP store opened at the Chelsea Warehouse in Manhattan. By closely managing the business, Barneys New York has maintained the standards of quality and service that has served as the company's guiding principles since its beginnings.

comme des garçons
comme des garçons
5th floor
clements ribeiro
5th floor
susan cianciolo
5th floor
marni
5th for
olivier theyskens
5th floor
dolce & gabbana
4th floor
accessories
main floor
shoes
4th floor

*High standards of quality and service has always been
Barneys guiding principles*

Macy's Herald Square

Macy's Herald Square

On October 28, 1858, R.H. Macy opened a small fancy dry goods store located on the corner of Fourteenth Street and Sixth Avenue. It was the beginning of a business which would grow to compete with the most prestigious and established of retailers. Some 44 years later, in 1902, the store moved to the present Herald Square location which has since become one of the busiest intersections in New York City. With the completion of the entire Seventh Avenue expansion in 1931, Macy's Herald Square became the "World's Largest Store," with more than 1 million square feet of retail space and is today, the third most visited New York City landmark.

Yet, Macy's isn't *just* a retailer.

Ingrained in the minds of New Yorkers and visitors alike, Macy's has truly become the authority on holiday fun and fantasy. Beginning in 1924, the Macy's Thanksgiving Day Parade™ has become a time honored tradition synonymous with the Thanksgiving holiday, the beginning of the Christmas season and a favorite for family festivities. Some 52 years later, Macy's also became the authority on Independence Day Fireworks. Since 1976, the Macy's 4th of July Fireworks™ Spectacular has rocked the city and the nation with brilliant light, color and sound.

Whether you're 100 years or 1 month old, there is clothing for everyone at Macy's Herald Square. Men, women and children can find an outfit for every occasion. Shop amongst the hottest names with the latest trends from DKNY, CK Calvin Klein, and Tommy Hilfiger. Or if the traditional brands for a truly classic look is more your style, Macy's also carries Polo by Ralph Lauren, Charter Club, and Jones New York. Almost everything that is needed for the home can be found at Macy's with extensive collections of small kitchen appliances, cookware, linens, china and more.

Sometimes we all just want a little pampering or need a little help finding that special something. The staff of fashion consultants at *Macy's By Appointment (MBA)* can help anyone pick out an unforgettable dress for a special occasion or an entirely new wardrobe. Both men and women have their own consultants to help coordinate wardrobes while the home accessories experts can guide the shopper throughout the home collections.

Macy's wants everyone's stay in our hometown to be a happy and memorable one. Located on the 34th Street Balcony Level, the *Visitors Center's* (VC) multi-lingual staff is always eager to welcome both tourists and native New Yorkers alike. Notify the VC in advance of a group's visit and they will coordinate store tours and fashion shows or plan special seminars and services geared toward specific interests. The staff can also even help reserve tickets for theater or sporting events, book tables at restaurants, provide subway maps and most importantly, help customers find their way around New York!

Macy's Herald Square has events happening throughout the year, from fashion shows to celebrity personal appearances. Call (212) 494-2442 to find out what is going on during your visit to the Big Apple!

Stop in, say hello, and have a wonderful visit to our hometown!

MACYSPORT

Macy★s Thanksgiving Day Parade

Diamond District

The world of 47th Street from Fifth Avenue west to the Avenue of the Americas

In the heart of Manhattan a world exists that is very different from anything else in the United States. It is a world that is only slightly more that 600 feet long, yet it has maintained a lifestyle that is unique and dates back to ancient times. It is a glittering fantasy land where billions of dollars worth of fine diamonds and other gems are bought and sold.

This is a world of 47th Street, from Fifth Avenue west to the Avenue of the Americas. It is the heart of the multi-billion dollar diamond business, handling more than 90 percent of all jewelry grade diamonds sold in the United States.

Sometimes referred to by the media as the "Streets of Diamonds" 47th Street is also known among diamond people as the "The Street". From the diamond shaped lighting fixtures at both ends of the street, the block is jammed with individual stores and exchanges, their windows ablaze with shimmering diamonds and fine gems.

The diamond business in New York began in the late 1800s and early 1900s.

The first diamond merchants, most of which were European Jews, set up shops in Lower Manhattan, first on Maiden Lane and then on Canal Street. By the mid 1920s, a thriving diamond industry had been established, that was know as the "The Diamond District".

In 1931, the Diamond Dealers Club was founded. It was originally located on Nassau and Fulton Streets. As some dealers became more affluent, they were able to set up offices in mid-Manhattan as close as they could get to the luxury stores on Fifth Avenue. The block of West 47th Street between Fifth Avenue and the Avenue of the Americas was the ideal choice.

When Hitler and the Nazis overran Belgium and the Netherlands, the diamond dealers of Antwerp and Amsterdam fled. Many eventually arrived in New York. By this time more diamond dealers from downtown had moved uptown. In 1941, the Diamond Dealers Club moved "uptown" to 47th Street.

A shrine to American individualism, 47th Street's hub is the Diamond Dealers Club. It is the most powerful organization in the nation's diamond business, often handling disputes among the constantly changing tableau that is 47th Street. Today, more than 20 languages are spoken on 47th Street and dealers now represent virtually every nationality.

Now celebrating its Diamond Jubilee, "The Street" remains unique, and behind this diamond curtain lies an exciting and exotic world where diamonds and other fine gems are displayed and sold, often at the best prices in town.

Among the 2,600 dealers, cutters and manufacturers who are based on 47th Street, competition is fierce. And yet, the entire system operates on a simple, strict code of honor: a person's word is his bond. Millions of dollars worth of stones may pass on consignment from one dealer to another, with nothing to record the transactions but a handshake. As a result, many of today's dealers are second, third and fourth generation diamond merchants with customers who return year after year, introducing new generations to the glittering wonders of 47th Street.

"The Street" is a glittering fantasy land where billions of dollars worth of fine diamonds and other gems are bought and sold.

Gift Organic

A refreshing Change

A onetime junk food addict, who reformed for health reasons, Cheryl Roth founded Gifts Organic as proof that living an organic and natural lifestyle is not about having to give up style, taste and decadence.

Presenting artfully packaged gifts and gift boxes that cater to the healthy needs of many New Yorkers and out-of-towners alike, Gifts Organic is a distinctive gift company that offers delicious delicacies, blissful baby and personal care products all prepared without chemicals, pesticides and free of refined and artificial ingredients. Along with harmonious accessories and usual things for the home, this inspired concept in gift giving proves that things do not have to be bad (for you) to be good!

Yes it's true; there is a way to balance indulgence with well-being. In other words, you can have your cake and eat it too. Not to mention your brownie, chips, cinnamon shortbread, caramel popcorn, chili or even macaroni and cheese.

Gifts Organic has a passion for healthy food and is constantly seeking the world to find the best in natural and organic products to suit even the most discriminating palate and taste. We also include our discoveries in earth-friendly products for home, bath and body, all so pure and finely-crafted

> "People who expect organic treats to be little more than prettied up rice cakes are in for a big surprise."
>
> **Cheryl Roth**
> *founder Gifts Organic*

that they too, are good enough to eat.

Whether its something indulgent for *the home* — colorful hand-crafted sculptural glass dinnerware, mother of-pearl serving pieces, contemporary lifestyle books on dairy free cooking and alternative healing; *the baby* — honey suckle baby bath, pansy flower shampoo, natural fiber baby blankets; the friend -aromatherapy body gels, mineral and vegetable bath soaps, feng shui jewelry or, just to tempt someone wi luscious organic and natural foods like freshly baked cookies (made specifically for Gifts Organic and so unbelievably delicious that you'll have to keep some for yourself!) and dairy free chocolates, Gifts Organic searched for and brought together products that infuse style, energy and healthy pleasure.

With the company's vast collection of food and gift items, Gifts Organic will cater to any special need, dietary guideline or allergy, be it Vegan, Vegetarian, Kosher, wheat free, dairy free or a guiltless gourmet its no wonder a number of well known

celebrities and fashion models who can appreciate the health and energy benefits of an organic and natural diet are frequent shoppers of this incomparable gift company.

Additionally, Gifts Organic offers a wonderful Healing Collection and Extended Get Well packages that provide a thoughtful way to show your support to a sick or chronically ill friend or loved one. Gifts Orgarnic will work with you to create highly personal care packages intended to foster wellness in body, mind and spirit.

It's truly the perfect balance between hip and wholesome - decadent and natural - glamour and good for you.

For more information on alternative healing, guiltless gourmet foods and combining hip with wholesome visit www.giftorganic.com. A natural, contemporary source of information on the latest and greatest trends the organic industry; tips on how to stay healthy while fighting the aging process naturally and remarkable insights on looking and feeling your best.

1-800-651-4438
cheryl@giftsorganic.com
www.giftsorganic.com

Gifts Organic takes pride in supporting City Harvest

To the left

Rhapsody Gift Bag - Let them unwind, uplift and get refreshed with this matchless gift bag complete with pure glycerin soap, body oil to renew silkiness, reviving aromatherapy candles, cocoa tea to indulge and to easily restore the senses - even while working. We also included Wet Suit Shower Wash in a refreshing blend of Ginger and Pink Grapefruit - it hydrates your skin while it awakens your senses. It's rhapsody without the resort!

Groovy Martini Box - A virtual party in a Box! Classic votive candles. Smooth Rain Organic Vodka and Olives accompanies by cutting edge stainless steel Martini Glasses and Shaker all perfectly paired with a jigger of jelly beans. Shaken or stirred - you'll be the toast of the town!

To the left

Got rice Milk? They'll dive into cookies so rich and chewy (and believably organic) they may never come up for air. Our made to order cookie box is filled with a variety of home made Chocolate Chip, Oatmeal Raisin, and White Chocolate Chip Chocolate Cookies all so tempting you may have to order an extra box for yourself.

141

The NBA Store

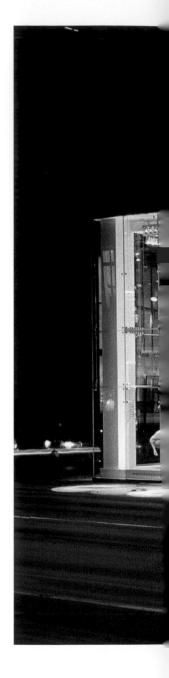

Sports fans from around the globe know that their destination of choice is the NBA Store, located on Fifth Avenue at 52nd Street in Manhattan, now in its third year as the ultimate basketball shopping experience. Beyond offering the world's most comprehensive collection of NBA and WNBA merchandise, the NBA Store brings fans up close to their heroes with regular in-Store appearances by some of the biggest names in sports and entertainment.

Covering 35,000 square feet on two retail floors, the Store enhances its more than 18,000 items and apparel for sale with a staggering range of multimedia driven attractions that draw on the extensive archives and creative abilities of NBA Entertainment - the league's global entertainment-media company whose properties include television, film, video, Internet, publishing & digital photography, consumer products, marketing partnerships, media properties and event relationships.

The NBA Store offers something for everyone, as merchandise from every NBA and WNBA team is available, along with the league's line of exclusively NBA Store-sold NBA logoman

apparel. Other merchandise includes personalized authentic jerseys and an exclusive line of NBA-branded sportswear from jewelry, collectibles, photography, artwork and gifts.

As shoppers enter the Store they are presented with a dramatic 170-foot-long arena-styled circular ramp to the lower level which features an ever-changing selection of NBA memorabilia. Fans wanting to work on their game can practice at the Store's shooting cage or grab something to eat at the Hang Time Cafe which serves game-style food such as soft pretzels, popcorn and hot dogs.

Monitors throughout the Store, including an arena-sized Jumbotron video board, air exclusive NBA and WNBA footage, live game broadcasts and NBA.com TV- the league's 24-hour digital television network.

For the 2000-01 season, the Store serves as the set for "The NBA Beat," the first-ever professional sports league interactive talk show, airing live from the Store's Fifth Avenue window front. The show is broadcast weekdays from 6:00 pm - 8:00 pm on NBA.com TV, and is webcast via streaming audio on NBA.com - the official Web site of the NBA. Fifth Avenue shoppers are welcomed to participate in the show by asking questions and giving their perspective on league issues live from the Store, send e-mail on NBA.com or call into the NBA.com TV studio.

Tune in to the NBA Beat presented by Sportsline - a live interactive talk show - weekdays from 6 pm - 8 pm ET on NBA.com

NBA.com additionally offers fans a one-step shopping place to get official NBA merchandise. The league recently launched its expanded e-commerce site, The NBA Store on NBA.com. The site provides fans with the most comprehensive assortment of exclusive NBA and WNBA apparel, electronic games and sporting goods in one place. Through specially designer individul team shops, fans can purchase a selcetion of merchandise from all 29 NBA teams and 16 WNBA teans in addtion to NBA and WNBA Playoffs, Finals and All-Star products.

NBA Store hours are Monday through Saturday 10:00 a.m. to 7:00 p.m., and Sunday 11:00 a.m to 6:00 p.m. with extended hours during the summer and holiday seasons. For more information on the NBA Store or to book a special event contact 212-515-NBA1, or visit www.nba.com / www.wnba.com.

The NBA Store on Fifth Avenue, with two floors of interactive entertainment in the heart of Manhattan, is the ultimate destination for basketball fans everywhere.

The Store regularly hosts free events for fans and families ranging from NBA stars and mascots, celebrity appearances, and concerts by today's hottest recording artists.

Shoppers can get anything from authentic jerseys, shorts, and even socks to the incredibly popular Hardwood Classics line of vintage NBA apparel.

Wonderland of the Wild and The Peninsula

Bronx Zoo's Rainey Gate in the Snow
Photo by: *D. Shapiro © Wildlife Conservation Society*

Bronx Zoo
Wildlife Conservation Society

Indian Peafowl
Photo by: *D. Shapiro © Wildlife Conservation Society*

The Bronx Zoo is a wonderland of the wild to be enjoyed at any age. The facility is beautifully designed and is located over 265 acres. It is the largest urban zoo in America and has great support with an annual attendance of approximately 2 million to date.

The grounds were opened to the public in 1899 and today the original site remains the headquarters for the *Wildlife Conservation Society (WCS)*. The Bronx Zoo serves as an international center for environmental education, wildlife health sciences, research, and conservation programs. The Bronx Zoo has developed award winning wildlife science curricula, including *Wildlife Inquiry through Zoo Education: WIZE* a nationally distributed environmental program which has been adopted by schools and wildlife centers in 46 states and several foreign countries. The Bronx Zoo Education Department also sponsors ongoing international initiatives.

The Bronx Zoo is home to more than 4,000 animals of 530 species, including Siberian tigers, Asian elephants, lowland gorillas, snow leopards, American bison and many more rare and endangered species. Each year the Bronx Zoo is witness to several hundred successful births and hatchings. Special habitats have been created for species ranging from snow leopards to birds of paradise. Animals are cared for in naturalistic exhibits including the Congo Gorilla Forest, Wild Asia, Jungleworld, Himalayan Highlands, World of Birds, African Plains, Baboon Reserve, World of Darkness, and World of Reptiles.

The Bronx Zoo has been a guiding force in the collaboration among accredited zoos in North America to preserve endangered species through the American Zoo and Aquarium Association's Species Survival Plan. Bronx Zoo staff play leadership roles in this multi-institutional program, which is directed toward careful and coordinated breeding management, supporting the preservation of animals that are losing their homes in nature. As Species Survival Plan coordinators, Bronx Zoo staff is involved in monitoring the genetic and demographic management of the entire North American captive population of many species. WCS field studies in Mongolia and China have complemented highly successful the breeding of snow leopards. Another successful project supported by WCS is the radiocollaring of forest elephants in Cameroon and the Democrat Republic of Congo in order to track their migrations. This research provides vital information at international conventions to support the declaration of this African elephant as an endangered species.

The purpose of WCS, since its founding in 1895 as the New York Zoological Society, has been to save endangered wildlife and their threatened habitats, and to inspire people to care about our natural heritage. Today, over a hundred years later, WCS has established more than 100 wildlife sanctuaries around the world, has led the crusade to protect over 90 million acres in 11 countries, and manages more than 300 field conservation projects in 53 nations.

"Animals are such agreeable friends — they ask no questions, they pass no criticisms. "

George Eliot

Adult Female Lowland Gorilla in Congo Gorilla Forest
Photo by: *D. DeMello © Wildlife Conservation Society*

King Vulture
Photo by: *D. DeMello © Wildlife Conservation Society*

Australian Lace Monitor Lizard
***Photo by:** D. DeMello © Wildlife Conservation Society*

Siberian Tiger licking whiskers
Photo by: Bill Meng © Wildlife Conservation Society

Snow Leopard leaping in snow
Photo by: *Bill Meng © Wildlife Conservation Society*

Wild Mongolian Horses
Photo by: *D. DeMello © Wildlife Conservation Society*

Red Panda in Himalayan Highlands
Photo by: D. DeMello © Wildlife Conservation Society

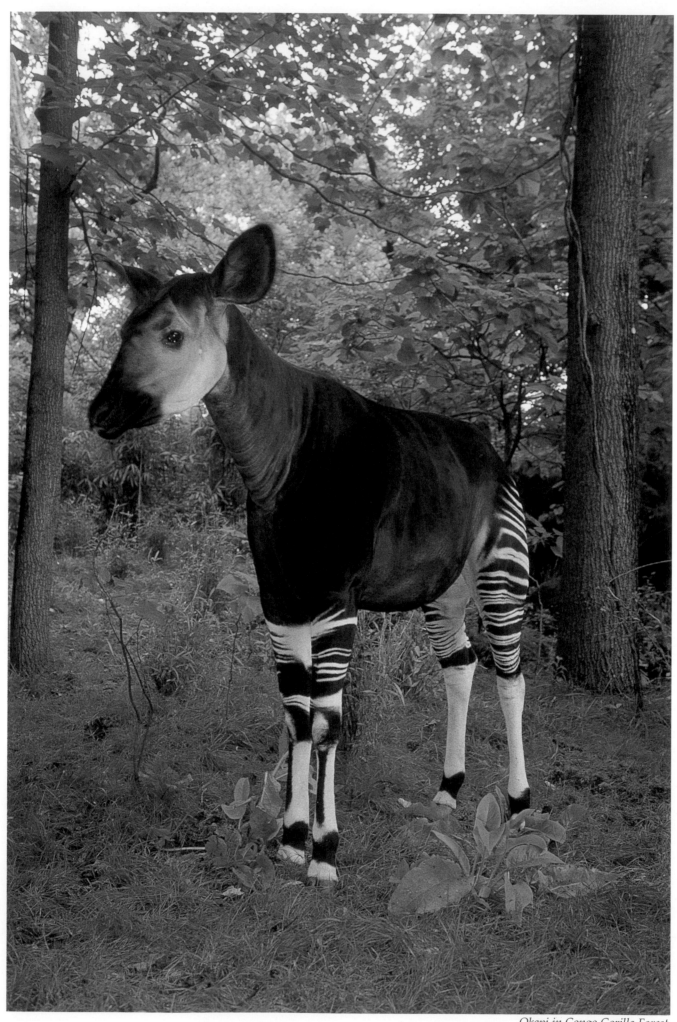

Okapi in Congo Gorilla Forest
Photo by: *D. DeMello © Wildlife Conservation Society*

Frog Beetle
Photo by: *D. DeMello © Wildlife Conservation Society*

Jamaica Bay Wildlife Refuge

Great Egret
Photos by: *Don Riepe/NPS* ©

The Jamaica Bay Wildlife Refuge is one of the most important urban wildlife refuges in the United States. Encompassing 9,155 acres, it is comprised of diverse habitats including salt marsh, upland field and woods, several fresh and brackish water ponds and an open expanse of bay and islands - all located within the limits of New York City. In addition, the district includes the North Channel Bridge area, Spring Creek, and a small recreational area, Frank Charles Park in Howard Beach.

The wildlife refuge is nationally and internationally renowned as a prime birding spot where thousands of water, land and shorebirds stop during migration. More than 325 species have been recorded here during the last 25 years. People visiting the refuge should stop at the visitor center to obtain a free permit and to learn more about the refuge.

In 1953, Park Dept. employee Herbert Johnson was transferred to the site and became the first refuge manager. Under his capable supervision and dedication, the barren landscape was transformed into a haven for birds and other wildlife. Trees, shrubs and grasses were planted to provide year-round food and shelter and a trail system was established.

In 1972, management of the refuge was transferred to the National Park Service as part of Gateway National Recreation Area. Gateway also includes Riis Park, Fort Tilden and the Breezy Point tip in the Rockaways; Great Kills and Miller Field in Staten Island; Floyd Bennett Field, Plumb Beach Dead Horse and Canarsie Pier in Brooklyn; Sandy Hook, in New Jersey - a combined total of 26,000 acres.

The refuge was initially "created" and managed by the N.Y.C. Parks Dept. In 1951, Parks Commissioner Robert Moses, after consultation with the U.S. Fish & Wildlife Service, ordered the creation of two large fresh water ponds, today known as the East Pond (120 acres) and the West Pond (45 acres).

From its inception, the refuge was managed to provide a variety of habitats to accommodate a diversity of wildlife species. Songbirds and small mammals find food, shelter and nest sites in the upland woods and gardens; egrets, herons, ibis and waterfowl utilize salt marshes and ponds.

In 1980, refuge staff initiated a program to introduce native species of reptiles and amphibians representative of disappearing or extirpated local fauna. Several small fresh water ponds were placed in up land areas as breeding sites for Spring Peepers, Green Frogs, and Painted Turtles to

West Pond, North Garden

name a few.

Also in 1980, the South Field Butterfly and Wildflower Management Zone was established. Over the past few years, plantings were established to attract butterfly species. Buddleia, Lance-leafed Coreopsis and Common Milkweed, add fragrance and color as well as provide a nectaring source for these beneficial insects.

An active nest box placement program added much needed cavities for tree swallows, house wrens, kestrels, barn owls and bats. The barn owl boxes have been especially productive for this magnificent raptor. Over 50 young were banded in 1986 and 1987.

People are also considered as part of the wild environment. Trails, benches, blinds, gardens and a visitor center provide "habitat" for humans.

The refuge visitor center, located on Crossbay Boulevard. in Broad Channel, Queens, provides a variety of services and information for the general public.

Boat in Marsh

Snow Geese

Breezy Point, Tern Colony
Photos by: *Don Riepe/NPS* ©

Sunset at Jamaica Wildlife Refuge

Monarch Goldenrod

Protected Shoreline

Sanderlings

Manhattan Skyline

Great Blue Heron
Photos by: *Don Riepe/NPS* ©

Rabbits Foot Clover (with Deptford pink)
Photos by: *© Don Riepe/NPS*

Rosa Rugosa

Cactus Blossom

Rosa Rugosa

Rock jetties provide for good, but slippery,
fishing spots for striped bass and blues
Photo by: *Kate Judge*

Riis Park, part of Gateway National Recreation Area, and its famous bathhouse draw scores of visitors to its pristine beaches

Fall-blooming Golden Rod and native dune grass brighten the many dunes in Ft. Tilden, Gateway National Recreation Area. The Ft. Tilden Natural Dune System is an expansive, ever-growing and highly protected area designed to stabilize the beach.
Photo by: *Kate Judge*

National Parks Rangers provide information on
how nature can exist in harmony with urban life
Photo by: *© Don Riepe/NPS*

Solace & the City
A view from the Rockways
Photo by: © *Don Riepe/NPS*

Waiting for Summer
Photo by: *Kate Judge*

The unbelievably beautiful sunsets not only draw amateur and professional photographers, but often lure even the most seasoned residents to view the awesome and vivid color shows.
Photo by: *Mike Deutsch*

Mural painting, "The Deep", is one of a series of three murals painted by local artist, Esther Grillo, with the help of local school children. The mural is painted on a concrete structure designed as a bus stop for the 1939 World's Fair. These structures resemble waves making them perfect easels for creative artists.

Photo by: *Kate Judge*

A view of Rockaway from one of the two bridges to the Peninsula
The apartment buildings boast "a view from every room"!
Photo by: *Kate Judge*

The Marine Parkway Gil Hodges Memorial Bridge serves as a romantic arena for evening boating and fishing.
Photo by: *Mike Deutsch*

Pilings remaining from old wooden jetties stand proudly
at low tide in the Sparkling Atlantic Ocean.
Photo by: *Kate Judge*

Unparalled Majesty!
Photo by: *Mike Deutsch*

Birds, mechanical & natural, enjoy a flight along the Rockaway shoreline
Photo by: *Kate Judge*

The Cross Bay Veteran's Memorial Bridge resembles a strand of jewels as it spans a serene Jamaica Bay. The bridge spans connecting Rockaway to the mainland also provide excellent crabbing possibilities.
Photo by: *Mike Deutsch*

The Historic Aircraft Restoration Project **(HARP)** is housed in Hangar B at Floyd Bennett Field, Gateway National Recreation Area.

Volunteers of varying age groups work and share their experiences and expertise while restoring numerous historic aircraft. **HARP** *is designed to help narrate the long and fascinating history of the once bustling airport.*

Photos by: *Kate Judge*

Queens Botanical Garden

Welcoming more than 300,000 visitors each year, the Queens Botanical Garden (QBG), in Flushing, is a gathering place "where people, plants, and cultures meet." This 39-acre oasis of unsurpassed beauty and tranquility is located in the heart of New York City's largest borough, just outside the northeast corner of Flushing Meadows Corona Park.

As the only source of botanical and horticultural information serving our nation's most ethnically diverse county, the Garden presents collections, seasonal displays, programs, exhibits, and events for an audience that speaks more than 130 languages and dialects, but can, at QBG, share the common language of horticulture. Through collections, education, and research initiatives designed to be accessible to all, QBG is realizing its vision "to be the botanical garden noted for presentation of plants as unique expressions of cultural traditions."

Queens Botanical Garden was born as "Gardens on Parade," a spectacular five-acre horticultural exhibit at the 1939-1940 New York World's Fair featuring some of the most innovative botanical displays to be seen at that time. With the onset of World World II, however, the once glorious gardens were allowed to become overgrown, and the exhibit remained in a state of disuse, virtually forgotten. In 1946, a group of civic-minded residents approached then Parks Commissioner Robert Moses about creating a botanical garden from the exhibit's designs and plantings left in place after the Fair. With his support they founded the Queens Botanical Garden Society, and developed a showcase of native and exotic plants and trees, with related programs in horticulture and ornamental floriculture, for area residents. QBG was opened to the public on June 5, 1948, as part of the borough's celebration of the 50th

anniversary of the consolidation of Greater New York. The Garden was later expanded to 20 acres.

With the advent of the 1964-1965 New York World's Fair, QBG and its collections were relocated across the street to a larger site. It took with it a number of plants and trees, including three blue Mt. Atlas cedars from the "Gardens on Parade" exhibit that currently grace QBG's Main Street entrance. The Unisphere and towers of the New York State Pavilion — icons of the 1964 World's Fair — can still be seen from atop the sloping hills of the Garden's 21-acre arboretum.

Sixty years after its debut to an international audience, QBG continues to serve a multiethnic audience year-round with a wide array of enjoyable educational programming, multilingual signage and publications, and public programs accessible to all. It offers free admission to visitors and charges nominal fees for children's and family programs. Eighteen acres of formal gardens include rose, herb, perennial, woodland, backyard, bird, and bee gardens; a Fragrance Walk; a pinetum; a wetlands exhibit; a Victorian-style Wedding Garden; and a compost home demonstration site. Seasonal displays feature more than 10,000 tulips, 1,400 rose bushes, annuals, perennials, and a Cherry Circle with flowering Kwanzan cherry trees and crabapple trees. A 21 acre arboretum provides recreational areas for visitors and community residents alike, as well as pedestrian access to Flushing Meadows Corona Park.

The Garden is a living laboratory for educational and cultural programs, which are designed to elevate the connection between botany and cultures and foster a sense of environmental stewardship among all those who participate in them. A Children's Garden program teaches budding horticulturist to

plant, tend, and harvest their own vegetables. Individuals age 60 and over tend a community garden and their own garden areas in the Senior Garden. More than 18,000 school children visit the Garden each year for programs; thousands more are served in off-site programs and videoteleconferencing. Guided and self-guided tours are offered to groups throughout the year; reservations are required.

QBG's Wedding Garden and Main Grounds serve as the setting for hundreds of wedding ceremonies and photographs each year. Facilities are also available for receptions, meetings, and other special events. Open

Wedding Garden
Photos by: © *Betsy Pinover Schiff*

seasonally, a Plant Shop offers a fine selection of indoor and outdoor plants, gardening accessories, books, and gifts for the gardener.

Queens Botanical Garden is just steps away from some of the finest Chinese, Korean, and South Asian restaurants in the metropolitan area. It is easily accessible by car, subway, train, and bus; parking is available in QBG's lot on Dahlia Avenue. The Garden is also a stop on the Flushing Meadows Corona Park trolley, which travels on weekends year-round to all of the park's cultural institutions and attractions.

All-America Selections Garden

American Museum of the Moving Image

Museum Entrance
Photo by: *Peter Aaron/ESTO*

The artifacts on display are drawn from the Museum's collection. With more than 83,000 items, the Museum has assembled the nation's largest and most comprehensive holdings of moving image artifacts, including photographs, licensed merchandise, video games, props, models, costumes, technical apparatus, fan magazines, posters, and much more.

The William Fox Gallery is devoted to temporary exhibitions exploring digital media. The current exhibition *Expanded Entertainment* explores the past, present and future of digital play, with games and other forms of interactive programming for computers and television.

In its Riklis Theater, Moving Image presents retrospective film series, often accompanied by discussions with the filmmakers. More that 400 screenings per year are presented, and the Museum works closely with archives, studios, distributors, and artists to ensure that films are shown as they were intended to be seen: in their original formats and in the best available prints.

The Museum's education program is one of its most vital components, serving more that 20,000 students per year in tours, screening programs, and science and math workshops. Curriculum-based education programs provide intermediate and high-school students with a clearer understanding of moving image media, and use film, television, and digital media to offer new perspectives on their study of English, History, Literature, Science, and Mathematics.

The American Museum of the Moving Image emerged from the efforts to save the historic Astoria Studios, one of the nation's leading film production facilities during the silent era and the early days of the talkies. The studio was built by Paramount Pictures in 1920 and used by the U.S. Army from 1942 until 1971. By 1977, it had been abandoned and was in a state of disrepair. To bring production back to New York, elected officials and leaders of the motion picture and television labor unions and guilds joined to form the Astoria Motion Picture and Television Foundation. The Foundation succeeded not only in returning the Studio to life but also in laying the groundwork for the Museum.

The American Museum of the Moving Image opened to the public in 1988. The first institution of its kind in the United States, Moving Image has been studied and admired worldwide for its innovative approach to exhibition design and its adventurous film, video and digital media programming.

The American Museum of the Moving Image explores the creative process behind movies, television, and digital entertainment. With lively, engaging exhibitions and programs, the Museum examines the innovation and artistry that make the moving image such a vital element of contemporary culture.

The core exhibition, *Behind the Screen*, is a dynamic environment that takes visitors through the process of producing, marketing, and showing movies and television programs. The exhibition includes more than a thousand historic artifacts, along with computer-based interactive experiences, commissioned works of art, demonstrations of professional equipment, and several hours of audio-visual material. With its elegant physical design and its integration of artifacts and interactive experiences, *Behind the Screen* offers a uniquely unified approach to its subject matter.

Doll Display
Photo by: *Peter Aaron/ESTO*

ADR (Automatic Dialogue Replacement) Booth
Photo by: *Peter Aaron/ESTO*

Astoria
A Colorful Change of Pace

Men Playing Bocce
Photo by: *Audrey Gottlieb*

It doesn't take long to sense Astoria's special character. Well-tended residential blocks criss-cross an international street life. The pace is neither Manhattan's hectic bustle nor the steady routine of the suburbs. Astoria is truly a village within the City, ideal for strolling, lingering and people watching.

Restaurants, cafes, bakeries and food shops are as close together as pastries in a box or olives in a barrel along 36th Avenue, Broadway, 30th Avenue, the western part of Astoria Boulevard (which leads to the Grand Central Parkway) and Ditmars Boulevard. Others are found on Steinway Street and tucked away on tree-lined side streets.

Large Greek-American and Italian-American populations have made Astoria a showcase of these cuisines, but many others are represented. A partial list would include: Adriatic, Afghani, Bangladeshi, Brazilian, Chinese, Columbian, Croatian, Cuban, Czech-Slovak, Ecuadorian, Eygptian, Filipino, Greek, Indian, Irish, Italian, Japanese, Lebanese, Mexican, Moroccan, Pakistani and Thai. Don't wait to try them. American and Continental restaurants, taverns, diners and ethnic fast food outlets add to this culinary kaleidoscope. Café-going is a special Astoria pleasure. Sip a refreshing beverage, eat a sweet or snack and read, chat or simply observe fellow café-goers and passersby (who will be doing likewise, in many languages). Astoria's cafés keep quite late hours and some offer live entertainment. Look for posted announcements as you explore.

There are many opportunities to take home a little Astoria. Bakeries, groceries and specialty food shops are chock full of authentic delicacies, many hard to find elsewhere (including more that thirty types of olives). Your eyes, nose and tastebuds will thank you.

Tired of riding elevators and escalators? "The World's Longest Department Store", Steinway Street is in fact a boulevard of bright stores and boutiques. As a Steinway Street shopper, you are just steps away from a wide selection of merchandise at attractive prices. Between 28th Avenue and 35th Avenue alone, numerous retailers specialize in electronics, footwear, furniture and apparel (men, women and children). Other popular categories are cards and party items, home decorating, jewelry and sporting goods.

The Steinway Street stop shared by the R and G subway Lines provides easy access to and from "The World's Longest Department Store." Once here, you can hop on the Q101 bus to go from one end to the other. Parking is available at "Muni-Meter" lots and on adjacent streets.

*A*nchoring three famous bridges - the Queensboro, the Triborough and the Hell Gate, this colorful corner of New York City has been a rural village, a retreat for the well-to-do, a company town for Steinway Pianos, and the movie industry's East Coast production center. Today, Astoria is a community where traditions from around the world are cherished and celebrated.

Astoria is easy to get to and get around. Broadway, 30th Avenue, 36th Avenue, Astoria Boulevard and Ditmars Boulevard (all stops on the elevated N line) run roughly east-west. Steinway Street, "The World's Longest Department Store" (A stop on the R and G lines), runs generally north-south. Along with Astoria Park and Athens Square Park, these "Main Streets" are often settings for festivals, fairs, parades and performances.

Italain Perfomer at Astoria Columbus Day parade
Photo by: *Audrey Gottlieb*

P.S.1

P.S.1 Contemporary Art Center

P.S.1 Contemporary Art Center in Long Island City, New York is a leading organization in the United States solely devoted to contemporary art and artists. P.S.1 is long distinguished for combining a cutting-edge approach to exhibitions and direct involvement of artists with the scholarly aspects of traditional museums, creating a unique resource for artists and audiences alike. Functioning as a living and active meeting place for the general public, P.S.1 is a catalyst for ideas, discourses and new trends in contemporary art. The New York Times said of P.S.1 in a recent editorial "It is less a museum than a place where art lives..." With its educational programs, P.S.1 assists the public in understanding art and provides the tools to appreciate contemporary art and its practices. Among the nation's art museums, P.S.1 is recognized as a defining force in the art world and is known for opening channels of communication between governments and the contemporary arts community. In 2000, P.S.1 became an affiliate of the Museum of Modern Art (MoMA). New exhibitions are presented throughout the year.

P.S.1 Contemporary Art Center was founded in 1971 by Alanna Heiss. P.S.1 (originally The Institute for Art and Urban Resources, Inc.) was primarily dedicated to the transformation of abandoned and underutilized buildings in New York City into exhibition, performance and studio spaces for contemporary artists whose innovative work was often disregarded by the city's museum establishment. From 1971 to 1975, the organization operated in a variety of locations throughout the city, including the Brooklyn Bridge and Anchorage, the 80th Precinct Building, the Coney Island Workspace, the Idea Warehouse, the Storefront and The Clocktower Gallery.

P.S.1 receives annual support from the New York City Department of Cultural Affairs towards operating costs. Programs of P.S.1 are supported by the New York City Department of Cultural Affairs, The Office of the President of the Borough of Queens, The Council of the City of New York, the P.S.1 Board of Directors, the New York State Council of the Arts, and the National Endowment for the Arts. Additional funding is provided by foundations, corporate and individual contributions, and membership and admission donations.

P.S.1 Contemporary Art Center is located just across the Queensboro Bridge from midtown Manhattan, at the intersection of Jackson and 46th Avenues, in Long Island City. It is easily accessible by bus and subway. Traveling by subway, visitors should take either E or F to 23 Street-Ely Avenue; the 7 to 45 Road-Courthouse Square; or the G to Court Square or 21 Street-Van Alst. They may also take the Q67 bus to Jackson and 46th Avenues or the B61 to Jackson Avenue. For information call (718) 784-2084 or www.ps1.org.

Richard Artschwager. Exit-Dont Fight City Hall, 1976/1997.
Ground floor hallway with electric lights.

P.S.1 Contemporary Art Center
Photo: *Clegg & Guttman*

Isamu Noguchi Garden Museum

Isamu Noguchi Garden Museum

*I*n 1961, Isamu Noguchi moved his studio and living quarters from Manhattan to a factory building in the industrial area of Long Island City, Queens. The new studio's proximity to marble and steel suppliers attracted Noguchi, who was working with these materials at the time. Long Island City has since developed as an arts community and continues to attract artists and arts organizations.

As he began to outgrow his storage space, Noguchi began to consider the possibility of expanding his facilities. In 1974, he was able to purchase an adjacent warehouse to serve as storage for the art works which he had held on to over the years. Originally a photoengraving plant, this 22,390 sq. ft. brick building was later to become the heart of the Museum's physical structure and home to the Isamu Noguchi Foundation, Inc.

In the years before the Museum opened, Noguchi began arranging sculptures, drawings and models in this warehouse. As the idea of opening this storage facility to the public began to take shape, Noguchi designed a unique, open-air, concrete gallery addition to the original brick building and landscaped the vacant lot to serve as a sculpture garden. A non-profit entity the Isamu Noguchi Foundation, Inc. was founded by Noguchi himself to manage this new museum, which opened to the public as The Isamu Noguchi Garden Museum (INGM) in May, 1985.

The Museum displays over 250 works by Isamu Noguchi. They include architectural models, stage designs, and drawings. The Museum is organized into 14 areas, and presents a complete retrospective of Noguchi's long and multi-faceted career. Visitors entering the Museum first confront the great stone sculptures of the artist's last years, carved in Japan and culminating his artistic odyssey. These are displayed in a covered area open to the elements, and in the garden for which the Museum is named. On the ground floor of this converted factory are exhibited more work in basalt and granite created in Japan during the last thirty years, marble pieces carved in Italy during the 1960s and 1970s, bronzes from the 1960s, and the great model of the unrealized "Memorial to the Dead of Hiroshima."

Upstairs visitors pass marble maquettes of "Slide Mantra," created for the 1986 Venice Biennale, before entering three galleries displaying smaller stone sculptures from the past thirty years. In the next area, detailed models and photographs document Noguchi's many landscape and architectural projects, and stage set elements and photographs present 11 of the 20 dance sets that he designed for Martha Graham between 1935 and 1963.

The artist's earliest works are shown in the penultimate gallery, beginning with brass and bronze sculptures done in Paris in 1928, through large brush drawings from Beijing and portrait heads done in New York during the 1930's, to the biomorphic sculptures of wood and stone that established Noguchi's reputation in the 1940's. The famous Noguchi table from that period leads to the last display area in the Museum, where a variety of his paper Akari lamps are exhibited. Altogether, the intimate and elegant displays introduce the public to an entire life of artistic activity, organized and presented as the artist intended.

Overview of the Isamu Noguchi Garden Museum

Socrates Sculpture Park

Arial View of Park - 2000

*L*ocated on the East River in Long Island City, Queens, Socrates Sculpture Park is an internationally renowned outdoor museum that also serves as a vital local park offering a wide variety of community services. In 1985, the area that is now Socrates Sculpture Park was an abandoned landfill. Filled with junked cars and garbage, the site was being used as an illegal dumpsite. Founded in 1986, Socrates was created by a coalition of artists and community members under the leadership of sculptor Mark di Suvero, a local resident. The work of hundreds of volunteers transformed this once-abandoned lot from a no-man's-land into a lasting community resource that is now a city park.

Socrates is open seven days a week free of charge and attracts over 35,000 visitors annually. The Park is a place where local residents can look at art, enjoy nature, walk their dogs, go fishing — and where their children can play. Others visit from around the world to view the ever-changing exhibitions of contemporary sculpture by some of the world's most renowned sculptors and some of the most promising new talents. Through its twice yearly exhibitions, its outdoor studio program and its fellowship program, Socrates has become a major New York City art institution forming, along with the Isamu Noguchi Museum, the Museum of the Moving Image and P.S.1, a vibrant burgeoning art scene in Western Queens.

The Park is the only public outdoor space specifically dedicated to both the creation and display of large-scale sculpture in the New York metropolitan area. Emerging, mid-career and established artists from around the world are invited to create new works on site and to exhibit those pieces in one of four exhibitions hosted each year. Over 300 artists have exhibited at Socrates since its inception. The Park also provides support to artists through grants, residencies and access to equipment and technical advisors. For many emerging artists, Socrates is their first opportunity make large work and to exhibit in New York providing a major

initial stepping stone for their careers. These artists go on to become artists that exhibit at venues around the country.

In recognition for its contributions to both the international art world and the local community in Queens, Socrates has received many awards including a 2000 Special Citation from the American Institute of Architects New York Chapter, and a National Recognition Award from the America the Beautiful Fund in 1998. The Park was named a "Great American Place" in 1995, selected as one of 63 specially recognized sites from around the country that are exemplary models of our built environment. In 1988 the City Club of New York awarded Socrates Sculpture Park the Albert Bard Award in Architecture & Urban Design and in 1987 the Park received a Doris Freedman Award from the Mayor of the City of New York for greatly enriching the public environment. The Park has also been recognized by the Art Commission of the City of New York with a 1985 special recognition award.

Socrates Sculpture Park provides outreach to the surrounding neighborhoods at senior centers, youth centers, hospitals and LIC/Astoria-area public schools. Through its education and visitors services programs, Socrates offers arts and educational workshops free of charge to over 1800 young people each year, tours to school groups and tourists throughout the year, and internship and apprenticeship opportunities to high school and college students. Socrates also provides direct financial return to the community by training and employing neighborhood residents.

Socrates Sculpture Park Inc. is a not-for-profit organization that receives a broad range of funding from individual, foundation, corporate and government sources. Socrates operates under an agreement with the NYC Department of Parks & Recreation to manage the land as a public park and sculpture space. With the support of the City through the efforts of Mayor Rudolph Guiliani, Queens Borough President Claire Shulman, Council Member Walter McCaffrey, and Parks Commissioner Henry Stern, Socrates has initiated a new series of improvements to provide even greater amenities for the community by expanding programming and outreach and improving its facilities. Some of the recent improvements to the Park are a handicapped walkway, electric service, a sprinkler system, a new street sidewalk and upgraded outdoor studio facilities for the artists who work on site.

Socrates Sculpture Park has been unique since its inception: it serves multiple purposes as a major art institution, a catalyst for economic development in the neighborhood, and open space allowing everyone access to the waterfront. Begun as one person's vision to transform a vacant lot, the park is a collaborative enterprise involving a diverse array of local residents, artists, and government agencies to create a valuable community resource as well as a vital cultural institution.

Park

Queens Wildlife

The Queens Wildlife Center is an 11-acre zoo that was originally opened in 1968 on the grounds of the 1964 World's Fair. The Wildlife Conservation Society (WCS) in cooperation with the City of New York renovated and reopened the zoo in 1992, and built upon the original American theme of the zoo. It now houses approximately 400 animals of some 40 species. A system of interpretive graphics and conservation education programs makes the Queens Wildlife Center an engaging celebration of wildlife and wild lands.

The zoo is designed to make both wild lands and wildlife a part of the park and a part of the American wilderness. Right off the pathway that leads visitors around the zoo are pockets of wild habitats, from the Great Plains to the rocky California coast, to a Northeastern forest.

A fascinating marsh exhibit incorporates aquatic plants and islands with ducks, geese, herons and egrets along with turtles to create a real marsh habitat. This area attracts native wildlife as well, and has become a prime bird watching site. Visitors can also see the special Sandhill crane, an attractive bird that is one of only two crane species native to North America. The presence of the bird here and explanatory graphics of their status in the wild, provide an important conservation message.

Two North American cat exhibits offer an intimate and close look at the bobcat and mountain lion(puma). The juxtaposition of the bobcats and the mountain lion exhibits and accompanying educational graphics, show the astounding differences between these exotic cats and the familiar house cats.

The aviary is a magical enclosure with a winding walkway that leads visitors from the forest floor with streams and ponds, to the treetops of this spectacularly planted aviary, to view native North American birds. The aviary is home to a variety of birds including cattle egret, black-billed magpie, wild turkey, several species of ducks and more recently red tailed hawks and turkey vulture.

A covered bridge provides a unique window into the world of the coyote, an adaptable survivor throughout North America. This exhibit help visitors understand more about one of New York State's most often misunderstood and most fascinating animals. The Roosevelt elk, the largest of the elk species in the United States herd, is also viewed from an interesting vantage point – an overlook-that is designed similarly to viewing areas in U.S. National Parks.

While the zoo's favorite sea lion exhibit blends into the surroundings and gives visitors the feeling that they are sharing a rocky California coast with the sea lions a few feet away. The zoo's "signature" species and exhibit is the American bison. This animal is an American symbol that was saved from the brink of extinction by WCS nearly a century ago. The bison range lets visitors glimpse at these magnificent animals from various points; the effect is that of seeing the Great Plains of long ago while traveling through the zoo.

Other fascinating animals that visitors will enjoy are the prairie dogs, South American spectacled bears and bald eagles. The bears offer endless entertainment as they hang out in their new specially made hammock, while the bald eagles continue to inspire awe.

The domestic area of the zoo offers the chance for young and old visitors to pet goats, sheep, llamas and other domestic animals. From these exhibits and educational graphics, all ages can learn the history of domestication of wild animals and plant species. This area also houses the Queens Education Department, with one of the large barns devoted to classroom space and special activities.

The zoo offers the chance for young visitors to pet domestic animals

USTA National Tennis Center

USTA National Tennis Center
Flushing Medows Corona Park
Photo by: *USTA*

n 1978, the United States Tennis Association turned a former World's Fair site into a marvel of public and private cooperation with the opening of the USTA National Tennis Center.

The USTA National Tennis Center is open to the public seven days a week, 11 months a year, closing only on Thanksgiving, Christmas and New Years Day.

Annual events held at the USTA National Tennis Center in addition to the US Open include the Eastern Wheelchair Tennis Championships and the Mayor's Cup high school tennis championships. USTA National Tennis Center staff conducts community tennis programs such as USA League Tennis, USA Team Tennis and USA Tennis 1-2-3. There are 33 outdoor and nine indoor courts available for public play. This does not include Arthur Ashe Stadium, Louis Armstrong Stadium or the Grandstand. Of the 33 outdoor public courts, the USTA built 11 in 1995 for use as practice courts during the US Open.

While the United States Tennis Association paid $285 million to build Arthur Ashe Stadium and to renovate Louis Armstrong Stadium and the grounds of the USTA National Tennis Center, the facility remains completely public. In fact, the USTA operates the USTA National Tennis Center for the city of New York and pays the city more than $400,000 per year in rent.

In January 1977, on a flight to New York to meet with the city parks commissioner, Hester glimpsed Louis Armstrong Stadium in snow-covered Flushing Meadows Corona Park as his plane approached LaGuardia Airport. From that moment, Hester's vision and perseverance led to the rapid development of site plans and agreements with New York City to create the USTA National Tennis Center. Ground was broken in October 1977, and remarkably, the new facility opened the following August, a mere 10 months later. By comparison, construction of Arthur Ashe Stadium took 30 months, from the initial groundbreaking in March 1995 to the August 1997 grand opening for Arthur Ashe Kids' Day.

There is a certain irony in having Arthur Ashe Stadium as the magnificent centerpiece of a tennis facility in a park that was once an ash dump. Flushing Meadows Corona Park, in fact is part of American Folklore as the site F. Scott Fitzgerald described as "the valley of ashes" in his 1925 novel The Great Gatsby.

But the site evolved from an ash dump at the turn of the 20th century to the center of the world attention within a few decades. Flushing Meadows Corona Park has been site of the 1939-40 World's Fair, temporary headquarters of the United Nations (1946-49), site of the 1964-65 World's Fair (at which time the Singer Sewing Machine Company built the Singer Bowl, renamed Louis Armstrong Stadium after New York City acquired the property) and now, home of the USTA National Tennis Center and the U.S. Open.

Venus Williams
***Photo by:** USTA/Russ Adams*

Queens Museum of Art

Panorama of New York City
The Worlds largest Scale Model

Panorama of New York City
The Worlds largest Scale Model

Queens Jazz Trail

While New Orleans is credited as "the birthplace of jazz", Queens, the largest of New York City's five boroughs, exerts a claim to being the home of jazz", chosen as the preferred residence of more leading jazz musicians than any other single place in the United States. Among these have been such immortal greats as Louis Armstrong, Dizzy Gillespie, Count Basie, Ella Fitzgerald, Lena Horne, Billie Holiday, Bix Beiderbecke, John Coltrane, Milt Hinton, Jimmy Heath, Fats Waller, Nat and Cannonball Adderley, Illinois Jacquet and a host of others, predominantly black, who gravitated there in the 1920-s, at a time when segregation barred, them from buying or renting homes in other suburban communities.

Led by singer Coby Knight, who grew up in Queens and was part of the team that uncovered the borough's jazz links, and jazz bassist Clyde Bullard, the Director of Performing Arts for the Flushing Council, the "Queens Jazz Trail" tours leaves from Flushing's landmark Town Hall, a handsomely restored Romanesque structure located at the corner of Northern Boulevard and Linden Place. There, at 10:00 A.M., tourists are loaded into mini-vans (soon to be supplanted by appropriately decorated trolley-busses) and given copies of a full-color souvenir map of the surrounding area with caricature portraits of the Queens jazz legends and drawings of their homes by noted illustrator Tony Millionaire. The five-hour escorted tour, part driving and part walking, precedes first to Corona, where the legendary trumpet players Louis Armstrong and Dizzy Gillespie, often thought to have been rivals, were actually close neighbors and friends. A stop is made at the modest red-brick house in which "Satchmo" lived with his wife, Lucille, from 1943 until his death in 1971 and which is now a National Historic Landmark, in process of being transformed into a museum. It was the Armstrongs' first home, after having lived most of their adult lives in

hotels, and though he could well have afforded an impressive manor in Beverly Hills or an estate on Long Island, Louis chose to settle down in a working-class neighborhood, where he often came out to play his trumpet for admiring groups of youngsters who gathered on his front steps. In Corona, Jazz Trailers are also shown the "Dorrie Miller" apartment complex that was home to saxophonist Cannonball and trumpeter Nat Adderly and is still the residence of saxophonist Jimmy Heath.

From there the tour continues past Shea Stadium and the old Louis Armstrong Tennis Stadium to the campus of Queens College, where a visit is paid to the Benjamin Rosenthal Library, housing the Louis Armstrong Archives. Highlights of the collection include five of Armstrong's trumpets and 14 of his trumpet mouthpieces as well as some 100 awards and plaques presented to him during his remarkable career, over 5000 photographs and nearly 100 scrapbooks. There are also 270 sets of band parts and 650 tapes recorded by Armstrong himself, who traveled everywhere with a reel-to-reel tape deck—the latter stored in boxes that Louis decorated by hand. The Jazz Trail stop at the Armstrong Archives allows time to listen to some of the tapes and watch a video including clips from Louis early television appearances as one of the first great celebrities of the twentieth century."

Jazz Trailers are taken south to beautiful Addisleigh Park in St. Albans, which has the highest concentration of jazz greats' homes in the borough and which saxophonist Illinois Jacquet once described as "a neighborhood to be proud of, a monument to black achievement". Walking through this community, one is shown the former home of Count Basie, a Tudor mansion with a backyard as big as a city block, on which an Olympic-size swimming pool was made available by "the Count" and his wife to neighborhood kids and was a favorite gathering place

for their barbecues and parties. The Addisleigh Park homes of vocalists Ella Fitgerald, Billie Holiday and Lena Horne, pianist-composer Fats Waller, trumpeter Cootie Williams, Duke Ellington's bandleader-son Mercer, the

Jacquets (Illinois and trumpeter Russell) and others are pointed out as the tour guides recall anecdotes about these colorful personalities. And when the 88 year-old bassist Milt Hinton is feeling "up to it", a visit with him and his wife, still living on 113th Avenue, is arranged.

Flushing Town Hall, at 137-35 Northern Boulevard, is easily reached by subway from Times Square or Grand Central in Manhattan via the #7 Train to Main Street stop, from which one walks north on Main Street to Northern Boulevard. The Long Island Railroad's Port Washington line from Penn Station also stops at Flushing Main Street and there are buses to the Town Hall from various parts of Queens on the Queens Surface Corporation lines.

Queens County Farm Museum

The striking interior of the farm house

The objective of the Queens county Farm Museum is to give the public an image of New York City's agricultural past. The history of the museum itself provides visitors the opportunity to learn more about the 200-year old site. Occupying the city's largest remaining stretch of natural, undisturbed farmland, the museum is part of a forty-seven acre parcel, made up of a landmark farmhouse and seven-acres of farmland.

The farm was owned by three families prior to being sold to the State of New York. Jacob and Catherin Adriance started the farm in 1772. The existing three-and-a-half-room home of the present farmhouse was built by Jacob, and is now the West Wing. The property was then sold to the Cox family in 1833. This family owned the farm until 1892. Under their ownership, they added what visitors know as the East Wing, which more than doubled the size of the farmhouse. In 1892, Daniel Stattel purchased the farm from the Cox family.

By 1900, it was the second-largest farm in Queens County. The State of New York bought the farm in 1927. The farm became part of the Creedmoor Psychiatric Hospital to provide fresh produce for Creedmoor's kitchen. It also provided therapy for its patients because patients helped raise crops and livestock.

During this period, Creedmoor built all of the present-day outbuildings, which included three greenhouses and a connecting potting shed, a wagon shed, two barns, garages, and a brooder house. The last major agricultural activity on the farm ceased in 1960 when the Creedmoor program was discontinued.

In 1973, the State declared this land a surplus. Local residents organized the Colonial Farmhouse Restoration Society of Bellerose in order to preserve the farm's historic structures and to operate the farm as a museum. Through their efforts, the farmhouse, along with seven acres of land encompassing the entire orchard, with its farmyard and outbuildings was declared a National and City Landmark, and the forty-seven acre site was turned into a city park (Adriance Farm Park).

The style of the farmhouse is Dutch. Inside the house, visitors will note original plank floors, beamed ceilings, flush horizontal-board wainscoting, raised-field paneling on the parlor chimney breast and two original doors. Some original plaster, window glass and hardware are noteworthy materials for having survived since the 18th century. With the entire exterior having been restored by the City of New York in 1986, the farmhouse is a striking building to visit.

Through tours of the museum, visitors can view the changing panorama of farm-life in all seasons of the year. The Queens County Farm Museum educates visitors about the history of farming in Queens by exposing the public to the basic facts of farm-life, whether it be by planted fields or grazing livestock. The public may visit the herb garden, the orchard, which covers about two acres of farmland, the chicken coop which houses 100 free-range laying hens, a cow shed, bee hives, planting fields, a duck pond, sheep pastures and a cow barn which is used for seasonal crop storage and animal care. A greenhouse also exists on the land and is operated by the Martin Van Buren High School Vocational Horticulture Program, but is not open to visitors.

By taking a tour of the Queens County Farm Museum, visitors can expect to learn a great deal about agricultural history in Queens. The surroundings differ from the well-known city life of New York, so it is a welcome change for the public.

The changing panorama of farm life during the winter season

An image of New York City's agricultural past

The Boys Choir of Harlem

Boys Choir of Harlem in Concert
November 17, 2000

Marriage of Figaro
New York Grand Opera
November 14, 1999

Nego Gato, The Wold of Brasil
March 9, 2001

Jimmy Heath
Legendary Saxophonist
October 20, 2000

Michael Sgouros • Eric Phinney • Yousif Sheronick • Trey Files

Ethos Heath Percussion Group
June 3, 2001

From Matter to Spirit:
Women Artists Facing the Millennium
March 25 - June 27, 1999

Albany

New York's

Imperial Capital

Donald W. Elliott Photography ©

Above
The Albany skyline from Rensselaer

Left
Sculling on the Hudson River by the Corning Preserve

View of Albany from Rensselaer
by William Hart 1846
Collection of Albany Institute of History and Art

Albany, the Capital of New York State, has been an important crossroads for nearly four hundred years. Henry Hudson reached the Albany Basin in 1609, and the area was settled by the Dutch in 1613. Albany is the oldest continually occupied city of the original thirteen colonies. Long coveted by European powers, the city was hotly contested over during the French and Indian Wars, and was the target of a major British invasion during the American Revolution, which culminated at the Battle of Saratoga in 1777. This victory for the American forces was the turning point of the conflict and led directly to recognition of the United States as a new nation. Albany became the Capital of New York State in 1788, which further enhanced the cities commercial importance, and gave it a preeminence in government affairs, which it maintains to this day.

In 1825 the Erie Canal opened

at the Port of Albany. The canal, the longest built since the Roman Empire, accelerated Albany's growth, and the city rapidly expanded to become a leader of the Industrial Revolution. The first railroad in the country originated in Albany in 1831, and within a few years had developed into the New York Central Railroad. During the American Civil War, Albany and the Capital District supplied a majority of the armaments, uniforms and materiel used by the Northern forces. After the war, Albany helped to rebuild the South with Adirondack pine, which was shipped down the Erie Canal and out of the Port of Albany. With the peace in 1866, the nation entered into an era of renewed greatness and prosperity. For the next forty years, Albany, as capital of the nations then wealthiest and most industrialized state, was transformed from a small provincial town into a city, which reflected the new imperial attitudes of the late nineteenth century. This incredible architectural legacy is Albany's inheritance, and is a delight to the visitor.

Albany from Mount Ida (Near Troy)
Engraving after the painting by
Asher Brown Durand, 1837

The New York State Capitol Building

Capitol Hill

The Capitol can truly be said to be the offspring of an uneasy marriage of architecture and politics. During its construction between 1867 and 1899, it had four different architects, each working in separate styles, although ultimately Italian Renaissance won out over the gothic. The Capitol is arguably the last great 19th century state capitol to be built in and around a city center. Lacking the dome and central rotunda which were planned but never realized, the three grand staircases became the focus of the design which is largely that of Henry Hobson Richardson (1876-1883), the most famous American architect of his day and who's Richardsonian Style profoundly affected Albany architecture. The interior staircases are currently undergoing extensive renovation and their respective skylights, blocked off for the past fifty years, will soon be uncovered and revealed.

Facing the city center is "The Million Dollar Staircase", named because of its astronomical cost at the time it was built. Completed during the final phase of construction (1883-1899), this cascading staircase is covered with a profusion of extraordinary and elaborate stone carvings of relief portraits, horticultural designs and even buffalo heads. These masterworks are largely the work of the British master craftsman, Louis J. Hinton, who later worked on the carvings in the Cathedral of All Saints in Albany.

At the foot of the staircase is the General Philip H. Sheridan Statue by John Quincy Adams Ward. Dedicated in 1916, this monumental equestrian statue depicts the Civil War general, who was an Albany native.

The Corridors of Power

Above
The Grand Senate Staircase

Below and Right
The antechamber and corridor leading to the New York Senate

Photographs by: Mark A. Brogna ©

The Nelson D. Rockefeller Empire State Plaza

Governor Nelson A. Rockefeller's lasting imprint on Albany, this colossal grouping of state office buildings has forever altered the city skyline. In keeping with the imperial image of the nineteenth century, Rockefeller wanted to bring state offices back into the city center, and construct a complex that impressed the observer with the State's power and grandeur. Wallace Harrison, the architect, had begun his career by working on the Rockefeller Center in New York City in the 1930's. In Albany, he created a vast space, known as the Empire State Plaza. The Plaza is elevated and separated from the city around it, and is linked to the State Capitol and the State Museum by way of a promenade nearly one third of a mile long, lined with alleys of maple trees and reflecting pools and fountains. Below the promenade is a three level parking garage, and a concourse of shops and restaurants. The Empire State Plaza includes the Justice and Legislative Office Buildings that flank the Capitol Building, the State Museum, Library and Archives, the New York State Theater and the forty-two story Erastus Corning Tower.

Photographed by: Lee Boltin

Donald W. Elliott Photography ©

Above
A Symphony concert at the Empire
State Plaza

Right
A young visitor enjoys the flowers

Left
Sculpture in The Empire Plaza
Trio, 1969 - 71 painted aluminum
10' x 32' x 13'10"
George Sugarman 1912-

Donald W. Elliott Photography ©

223

The Billboard 1966
Plaster, wood, metal, and rope
15'9" x 9'9" x 1'8"

George Segal
1924-

Governor Rockefeller, in recognition of the importance of the arts and the emergence of New York as the home of many of America's most innovative and talented artists, began plans for the Empire State Art Collection in 1961, and the first purchases were made in 1966. This collection features the work of artists who practiced in New York during the 1960s and 70s, and is the most important State collection of modern art in the country. It is also the largest collection of modern American art in any single public site that is not a museum. Works by Robert Motherwell, Clyfford Still, Jackson Pollock, Claes Oldenburg, Louise Nevelson

and Alexander Calder among others are represented here. In its embrace of abstract art, the collection positioned the State as a forward-thinking patron and its government as enlightened and advanced. Artists were intrigued by the immense out-door spaces in the thirty-five acre Plaza and accepted these sites as a challenge for their works.

The Empire State Plaza is a great place to visit. From the observation deck of the Corning Tower not only Albany, but the entire Capital District can be seen, and there are spectacular views of the Adirondack, Green and Catskill Mountains. The Plaza is also frequently used for outdoor concerts, festivals, and hosts wonderful fireworks displays on New Years Eve and the Fourth of July.

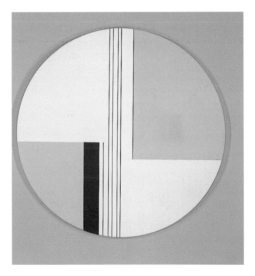

Top
Voltri - Bolton Landing Series
Volton XVIII, 1963
painted steel 9'2" x 5'4" x 1'3"
David Smith 1906 - 1965

Above
Large Tondo, 1969
acrylic on canvas 6'7" diameter
Ilya Bolotowsky 1907-1981

Left
Smoker, 1963
oil on canvas 5'10" x 6'4"
Philip Guston 1913-1960

State Education Building

The New York State Education Building, or "State Ed" as it is known locally, was the first major building to serve solely as a headquarters for education, and is one of the finest examples of beaux-arts architecture in America. This building is the incarnation of the vision of Andrew Sloan Draper, New York's aggressive first Commissioner of Education. Begun in 1908 and completed in 1912, it boasts the longest freestanding colonnade of Corinthian columns in the world. Designed by Henry

Photograph by: Mark A. Brogna ©

Hornbostel, the New York City architect noted for his Queensboro and Hells Gate Bridges, this temple of education housed for many years the State Museum, Archives and Library. The magnificent main reading room is modeled on that of the Bibliotheque Nationale in Paris, and its soaring fifty foot ceiling is spanned by Guastavino vaulting, resting on slender iron columns. On the granite steps of the Washington Avenue entrance, facing the Capitol, are two life-size bronze lighting fixtures by sculptor Charles Keck, depicting children absorbed in various artistic pursuits. The State Education Building has recently undergone an extensive interior restoration returning it to its original 1912 appearance, and it will soon become the new home for the Offices of Professional Licensing. It will be open for guided tours by appointment.

Left
The Grand Colonnade of the State Education Building on Capitol Hill
Right
Sculptor Charles Keck's bronze children gaze down from the monumental lamps on the steps of the State Education Building
Below
The facade of State Ed., viewed from the Capitol Porch

Photographs by: Mark A. Brogna ©

The Cathedral of All Saints

From the Collection of The Cathedral of All Saints

The Cathedral of All Saints was the first Episcopal cathedral in America to be conceived and built on the English model of church, hospital, convent and school. The brainchild of William Croswell Doane (1832-1913), first Bishop of Albany, the cathedral was intended to recreate and literally imitate its English prototypes, including the ancient pavements and stones. This was a radical departure from the then fashionable Gothic Revival Style, and represented a new American approach to architecture, in keeping with New York States imperial posture of the 1880s, and that of Albany in particular. The American Cathedral, as it came to be known, was the subject of an intense international design competition which was ultimately won in 1882 by the relatively obscure twenty-nine year old British architect Robert Wilson Gibson (1853-1927). The Gibson design was selected

Photographs by: Mark A. Brogna ©

over plans submitted by Henry Hobson Richardson, America's architectural darling, who's design had been prominently featured in Harper's Weekly.

Ground was broken in the summer of 1884 and work continued unabated until 1888, and again from 1903-1908. At slightly over three hundred and twenty feet, the structure was then the largest cathedral to be built in America. Although still incomplete, it now ranks fifth in the nation and twenty-eighth in the world in size. The cathedral contains mosaics attributed to Puvis de Chevannes, 16th century choir stalls from Belgium, and possibly the

largest section of 11th century Cosmatesque pavement in the world, outside of Italy. The cathedral is the only unfinished set-piece on Capitol Hill and the congregation is currently involved in a choir roof restoration project. There are also plans to replace the temporary roof, which was placed over the transept and nave nearly one hundred and twenty years ago.

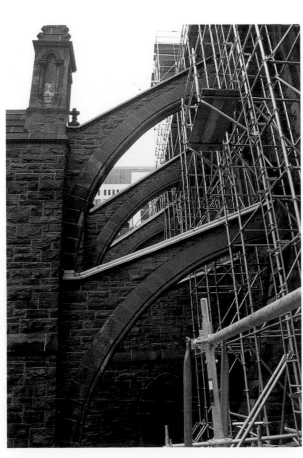

The cathedral contains some of the finest English glass in America with windows by Burlisson and Gryll, and Clayton and Bell of London. The windows in the baptistery are believed to be the earliest known memorial to Leland Stanford Jr., who's untimely death in Italy at the age of fifteen in 1886, led to the founding of Stanford University by his father, Leland Stanford, the Governor of California and an Albany native.

There are six important windows in the choir celestory which were designed by George Daniels (1854-1940) principal artist for Clayton and Bell of London and official stained glass printer to Queen Victoria. Daniels is widely acknowledged, together with William Morris, as a leader of the Arts and Crafts Movement, and was an influence on such artists as N.C. Wyeth, Maxfield Parish, and Arthur Rackham. The Daniel's windows in the cathedral, each nearly

George Daniel's glass windows glow in the Cathedral celestory.

Opposite Top
The Prophet Jonah

Opposite Bottom
The Agnus Dei panel

Left
The Prophet Moses

Below
The Prophetess

Photographs by: Mark A. Brogna ©

thirty feet in length, are believed to be the artist's most important commission outside of England, and were unrecognized until recently. The significance of the windows is enhanced due to the tragic loss of much of Daniels' work during the bombing of London in World War II. The cathedral is well worth a visit.

Academy Park

Donald W. Elliott Photography ©

Above
City Hall as seen from
Academy Park

Opposite Top
The old Albany Academy
designed by Hooker in 1808

Opposite Bottom
The New York State Court of
Appeals

The area around Academy Park, just below the Capitol, is one of Albany's most beautiful and historically significant spaces. While standing in Academy Park, and looking up at the Capitol, it is possible to see three buildings that define the best of two hundred years of American Architecture. The former Albany Academy, now the Joseph Henry Memorial, is Albany's oldest public building, and was designed by architect Philip Hooker in 1814 to house a boy's school. Hooker, like Bulfinch in Boston and Latrobe in Baltimore, was a classically trained local architect and surveyor, whose elegant Federal-style buildings defined the Albany skyline in the early nineteenth century. The beautifully designed cupola, with its arcades and pilasters, is very reminiscent of New York's City Hall, completed one year earlier in 1813. The park was laid out in 1833, and was the scene of the Army Relief Bazaar in the winter of 1864, that raised over $82,000 for the Union forces during the Civil War.

The New York State Court of Appeals was erected between 1832 and 1842 based on designs by Henry Rector, a pupil of Philip Hooker. It is one of the finest examples of Greek Revival Architecture in New York, as well as one of the earliest triumphs of historical preservation in America. In 1916, Lewis F. Pilcher, the State Architect, designed an addition to the building to accommodate an 1881 courtroom by Henry Hobson Richardson that was moved from the Capitol to the Court of Appeals. Not only the walls, windows and fireplaces of the Courtroom were moved, but also all of the decorative furnishings as well!

The Albany City Hall is considered by many to be Henry Hobson Richardson's

masterpiece. Constructed from Milford granite and Longmeadow brownstone between 1880 and 1883, it replaced a building designed by Henry Hooker that was destroyed by fire in 1880. The two hundred foot tower overlooks Capitol and Academy Parks, and contains a carillon of sixty bells installed in 1927, the first city carillon in the United States. A concert is played on the bells at noon on Fridays.

Photographs by: Mark A. Brogna ©

Washington Park

Albany's Washington Park, like Central Park in New York City, was conceived by Calvert Vaux and Frederick Law Olmstead, America's premier landscape architects. Olmstead also created the gardens and extensive park at Biltmore, the Vanderbilt estate in Ashville, North Carolina. Development of the park began around 1870, as the city began moving westward after the Civil War. The curving roadways, wooded glades and vistas of lakes and ornamental plantings are consistent with the Romantic and Esthetic movements ideal of the natural and gardenesque. The mature plantings date from the 1890's when the park was under the direction of William S. Edgerton, who for over thirty eight years continued Vaux and Olmstead's vision by saving old trees and constructing decorative pavilions and boathouses.

The Civil War Monument (Soldiers and Sailors Monument) dates from 1912 and dominates the northern entrance to Washington Park, facing elegant "mansion row" on State Street. Behind the large bronze figure depicting Peace, is a procession of more than sixty life-sized figures carved in marble in low relief. The memorial was restored in 1986, and is a popular spot in the park, in that it connects a beautiful tree-lined pedestrian promenade with the Moses Fountain on the parks southern end.

Washington Park's site has long been associated with Albany festivals. In the 17th and 18th centuries Pinksterfest, a week long celebration for the cities African-American population was held here, and the Albany militia drilled where the Lakehouse now stands. In the spring, Albany's Dutch heritage is remembered during the Tulip Festival, when more than one hundred thousand blossoms open, and a Tulip Queen is crowned. The park hosts numerous concerts, plays, athletic events and even large-screen movies throughout the year. During the winter holidays, the ancient trees are hung with a myriad of colored lights which transform the park into a magical wonderland.

Photograph by: Mark A. Brogna ©

Left
Snow covers the Civil War
Monument in Washington Park

Below
The Lake House under a clear
Autumn sky

Albany's varied architectural styles are reflected in the homes surrounding Washington Park

Mansion Row

The streets facing Washington Park display residential styles spanning the entire late Victorian and early Modern periods, and reflect Albany's importance as a major industrial and financial hub during the opulent decades following the Civil War. Some of America's finest 19th century homes surround Albany's historic Washington Park, and are some of the best examples of townhouse architecture remaining in the country. The city is fortunate to have had this entire area survive into the present day.

These distinguished residences were designed by local and internationally renowned architects including Henry Hobson Richardson, Sanford White, R.W. Gibson, Albert Fuller, and Marcus T. Reynolds.

Each house represents a uniquely different style, and their exteriors and interiors have, with few exceptions, remained as their creators envisioned them at the turn of the 19th century.

Photographs by: Mark A. Brogna ©

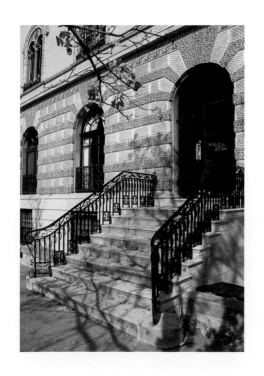

The State House
Morgan

The State House at 393 State Street, located on a quiet, tree-lined residential street overlooking Washington Park was the lifelong home of Alice Morgan Wright, who resided here from 1888 until her death in 1975. The house was designed by R.W. Gibson, the architect of the Cathedral of All Saints, for her father, Henry Wright, who made a fortune in dry goods during the Civil War. The multiple peaked gables and intricate interior details reflect Gibson's love of the Japonaise aesthetic of the 1880's, which presaged modern American art. Ms.

Photographs by: Mark A. Brogna ©

Above
The two-color rusticated brownstone facade of the Morgan State House glows on an Autumn afternoon

Right
Alice Morgan Wright (1881-1975) noted suffragette, artist & animal rights activist, life-long resident of 393 State Street

Smith College, Sophia Smith Collection

Wright was among America's most noted figures in obtaining women's suffrage who, after being jailed in London with Emaline Pankhurst, returned to New York where in 1921 she helped found the New York League of Women's Voters. An influential artist of the Art Deco style, Ms. Wright maintained a studio on the fourth floor of the house and her works may be found in museums and private collections throughout the country.

The property was purchased in 1995 by Charles E. Kuhtic, a local entrepreneur and designer, to create an executive inn. The inn provides luxury accommodations and customized services for its guests, in an atmosphere which leaves them feeling truly at home.

The Morgan State House has been voted "The Best in the Capital, Saratoga Region" for the past four years.

Left & Above
Architect R.W. Gibson's arched doorway and iron aesthetic lantern

Right Above
The grand staircase served as seating for musical evenings in the 19th Century

Right Middle
Once Alice Morgan Wright's Art Studio, now a spacious guest suite

Right
The Master bedroom fireplace reflects Gibson's Japonaise designs

Photographs by: Mark A. Brogna ©

Above & Below

Larkfest attracts
thousands of visitors
annually

Lark Street
"The Village in the City"

Below

One of the many
interesting shops
along Lark Street

Below

One of the many
interesting shops
along Lark Street

Photographs by: Mark A. Brogna ©

The Lark Street neighborhood is situated between "Mansion Row" on Washington Park, Capitol Hill and the downtown business district. As such, it is the perfect place in the city for people to live, meet and socialize. Within the neighborhood are more than seventy restaurants, bars, cafes and shops, housed in some of Albany's most historic buildings. The street serves as a stage for a number of art and music festivals year round, and every autumn the neighborhood celebrates "Larkfest". This event, presented by the City of Albany and the Lark Street Business Improvement District, recently celebrated its 20th year with food, music, and fun for the whole family. With an estimated 60,000 people in attendance, this event has become one of the largest outdoor events in Upstate New York, and is a great way to kick off the fall season in Albany's exciting "Village in the City".

The Lark Street BID has helped to recruit more than twenty new businesses, renovate the exteriors of more than thirty historic buildings, and provide essential programs of security and maintenance for the neighborhood.

Photograph courtesy of Lark Street. BID

Above
The Lark Street neighborhood features a unique collection of restaurants and shops nestled in Victorian era buildings

Collection of Albany Institute of History and Art
Photograph c. 1905

Above and Right

This Federal period building on the corner of Lark and State Streets has been a restaurant for nearly one hundred and seventy years

Photograph by: Mark A. Brogna ©

241

Downtown & The Waterfront

Donald W. Elliott Photography ©

Although the buildings of downtown Albany have changed dramatically over the past three and one half centuries, the pattern of narrow streets between Broadway and the Capitol still follow the same paths laid out in the early

Above
A painted medallion accentuates the beauty of Albany's historic Palace Theatre
Below Left and Right
The USS Slater and Henry Hudson's Half-Moon are popular waterfront attractions
Opposite Left
The traditional retail center of downtown Albany
Opposite Right
The old Delaware and Hudson Railroad Building (now SUNY Plaza), with it's copper weathervane, is one of downtown Albany's many architectural gems

settlement, and encompass a number of distinct historical neighborhoods. The Pastures and Mansion Districts are quiet enclaves of early nineteenth century houses, many in the Federal and Greek Revival style, located along the Hudson River on the cities south side. To the north, the Palace Theater, constructed in 1929 at a cost of 3 million dollars, has housed the Albany Symphony Orchestra since 1931. Its interior retains Austrian Baroque features, with decorative plaster and ceiling murals in the lobbies.

In 1912 the city hired noted urban planner Arnold W. Brunner of New York City to design a great plaza at the foot of Capitol Hill, that would link the waterfront and commercial districts with the government center. Reflecting the cities Dutch heritage, Albany architect

Marcus T. Reynolds, designed a massive building based on the 13th century Cloth Hall in Ypres, Belgium. The Delaware and Hudson Building, now the headquarters for the State University, was the result. The copper weathervane atop the central tower represents Henry Hudson's ship the Half-Moon.

Plans are now being implemented which will reconnect Albany's historic waterfront with the downtown area. A full-scale replica of the Half-Moon, as well as a W.W.II era destroyer, the U.S.S. Slater, can be visited on the Hudson River at the foot of State Street during the summer months.

Above
Jacks, a popular downtown
eatery since 1937

Photographs by: Mark A. Brogna ©

243

Saratoga

A thirty minute drive north of Albany, Saratoga Springs has been a premier summer destination for

centuries. Some have come to be a part of the excitement of the world renowned Thoroughbred track, others to "see and be seen". Others visit Saratoga Springs to partake of the legendary healing waters, to revel in the county's rich and varied natural beauty, to capture a bit of the past at the area's historical sites and Victorian mansions or to simply relax and enjoy.

Saratoga features year-round activities and attractions for adults and children. In addition to the summer race meet at Saratoga Race Course, there are other popular activities that the entire family

will enjoy. From museums to theater performances, to harness racing at the Saratoga Equine Sports Center, or taking in the area's extraordinary architecture, there are always plenty of fun and unique activities to do.

Saratoga was the site of the battle known as "the turning point of the American Revolution" in 1777. A visit to the Historical Society of Saratoga Springs Museum, to Grant's Cottage, or to the Saratoga Battlefield site and monument in the nearby town of Stillwater, will bring this rich history to life. The National Museum of Racing and Hall of

Top
Broadway in downtown Saratoga attracts many visitors with it's varied shops and restaurants

Above
The Canfield Casino in Saratoga's Congress Park once a gambling palace now hosts glittering social events

Right
The Saratoga Polo grounds host international competition during the racing season

244

Fame will excite both racing aficionados and first time enthusiasts. The museum recently underwent a multi-million dollar renovation and features two new galleries and more interactive exhibits. A second national museum in Saratoga Springs is the National Museum of Dance. Here, visitors can trace the history of dance from the traditions of its past, to the glorious present and exciting future. The Saratoga Performing Arts Center, an open air amphitheater, is the summer home of the Philadelphia Orchestra, the New York City Ballet, the Jazz Festival and many other classical and popular artists.

Above
World-class thoroughbred racing at the Saratoga racetrack

Left
The sun strikes the roofs of the historic grandstands during early morning exercise

Fire Works explode above the Empire Plaza
during the annual Fourth of July festivities
Photographs Donald W. Elliot Photography ©

Credits:

Author/Albany, The Imperial Capital
Edward Wallis Doucet, M.D.
399 State Street
Albany, NY 12210
E-mail: ndoucet@statehouse.cm

Photography
Mark A. Brogna
The Morgan State House
393 State Street
Albany, NY 12210
E-mail: mbstudios@statehouse.com

Donald W. Elliot
Donald W. Elliot Studios
37 Maplewood Ave
Albany, NY 12205
www.dwestudio.com

Layout Design
Charles E. Kuhtic
The Morgan State House
393 State Street
Albany, NY 12210
E-mail: ckdesigns@statehouse.com

Special thanks to:
Collection of Albany Institute of History and Art
The Empire State Collection
The Collection of The Cathedral of All Saints
Alicia Zumback, Stuyvesant Photo
The Saratoga Chamber of Commerce
Joe Cook, Moto Photo

Credits:

The Rockaways

The Wave
Emil Lucev, Rockaway Historian
Chamber of Commerce of the Rockaways, Inc.
Patrick Clark and Geoff Rawling, Rockaways Artists Alliance
Old Rockaway, New York by Vincent Seyfried & Wm. Asadorian

Special Advertising Section

THE REGENCY
A LOEWS HOTEL
NEW YORK CITY

IMAGINE A PLACE featuring twelve select suites

as unique as the months of the year. Where

distinctive styles from Soho chic to Sutton Place

panache, Gramercy grandeur to Park Avenue

prestige redefine luxury, and rejuvenate your soul.

Suite dreams are made of these.

Can you imagine it? WE DID.

THE GRAND SUITES

THE REGENCY

Park Avenue at 61st Street
Call 1-800-23-LOEWS • www.loewshotels.com

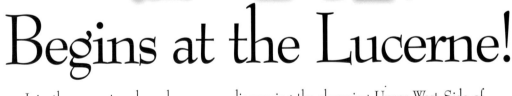

Design: Morris Berman Studio Inc.   Photography: Rob Kern

Excelsior

HERE'S ONE NEW YORKER YOU'RE GOING TO LOVE

What's not to love. We have everything. Great location, fabulous accommodations, incomparable service, truly superior public space and facilities, rates that are down to earth and, above all, an attitude that makes us Manhattan's most lovable New Yorker.

You'll love the fact that the New Yorker Ramada Inn & Plaza is the closest hotel to the Javits Center, near Madison Square Garden, the Empire State Building, Penn Station, the Garment Center, the Theater District, Macy's and all great midtown stores and restaurants.

The New Yorker Ramada Inn & Plaza features 1000 newly decorated rooms and suites as well as a luxury Tower where many of the rooms and suites have balconies and spectacular views. And our Fitness and Business Centers will keep you and your work in shape.

You can dine like a real New Yorker at our fine restaurant, La Vigna Ristorante & Bar. For early risers and night owls our Tick Tock Diner is open 24 hours. Or have a cup of coffee at our delightful lobby Espresso Bar.

But best of all, you'll find that this New Yorker is friendly, accommodating, courteous and ready to make your stay in Manhattan a total pleasure.

FOR RESERVATIONS: 1 800 764 4680

481 Eighth Avenue at 34th Street New York, New York 10001
212 971 0101 Fax 212 563 6136 www.nyhotel.com

the NEW YORKER
HOTEL
A RAMADA® INN & PLAZA

Discover the "O

Explore the art galleries in So

bistro in Tribeca.  Enjoy

winding streets of Greenwic

Little Italy, Ellis Island, The

or enjoy a dinner cruise arou

15 Gold Street, New York, NY • 1-800-Holiday or 212-232-7800 •

ther" New York

o.   Lunch at a French

reat shopping along the

Village. Visit Chinatown,

tatue of Liberty,

d Manhattan.

A PERFECT COMPLEMENT TO THE

UPPER WEST SIDE, ON THE AVE

HOTEL'S ACCOMMODATIONS INCLUDE

PENTHOUSE, KING AND QUEEN

ROOMS, ALL OF WHICH OFFER

GUESTS A UNIQUE OPPORTUNITY

TO ENJOY AN AUTHENTIC

MANHATTAN NEIGHBORHOOD.

ON THE AVE

HOTEL

2178 Broadway at 77th Street
New York, NY 10024
800-509-7598
www.ontheave-nyc.com

It feels great at the top.

SORRELL COMMUNICATION INC.

PUBLISHING • ADVERTISING • 4-COLOR WORK

7906 31st AVENUE • EAST ELMHURST • NEW YORK 11370 • USA
TELEPHONE: (718) 205-0665 • FACSIMILE: (718) 205-1061
E-MAIL: SORRELLCOMM@aol.com
WWW.SORRELLTHEBESTOF.COM

pumpkinmaternity

store
407 broome street
near lafayette, nyc
212.334.1809

mail order
800.460.0337
www.pumpkinmaternity.com
featured in vogue, bazaar & instyle

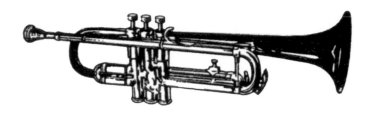

© Christine M. Douglas

Queens B

© Betsy Pinover Schiff

Open year-round. Closed Mondays, except legal holidays. Hours vary by season. Admission is free. Easily accessible by car, bus, subway, and the Long Island Rail Road. Parking is available in the Garden's lot on Dahlia Avenue.

otanical Garden

Where people, plants, and cultures meet

Enjoy 39 acres of beauty and tranquility in the heart of New York City's largest borough.

Featuring:

- 18 acres of formal gardens
- Seasonal displays of tulips, roses, annuals, and chrysanthemums
- Children's Garden program
- Free lectures, concerts, and special events year-round
- Guided and self-guided tours for schools and groups
- Weekend family programs
- Wedding Garden
- Plant Shop (open seasonally)
- New Fragrance Walk, Perennial Garden, and Wetlands Exhibit
- 21-acre arboretum
- Weekend trolley service to and from Flushing Meadows Corona Park
- Facilities for photographs, weddings, receptions, and events

Queens Botanical Garden

43-50 Main Street, Flushing, NY 11355
Phone (718) 886-3800   Fax (718) 463-0263
www.queensbotanical.org

Play Where the Champions Play!

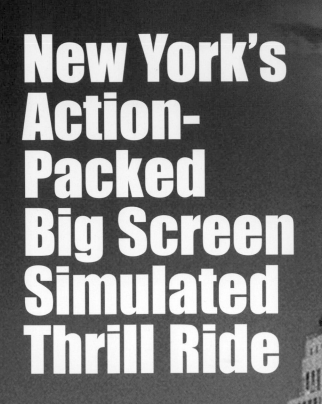

FLUSHING TOWN HALL

Your Ticket To The Arts!

CLASSICAL MUSIC

FAMILY PROGRAMS

OPERA

JAZZ

EXHIBITIONS

THEATRE

137-35 Northern Blvd.
Flushing, NY 11354
(718) 463-7700, x 222

275

The ocean is exciting, exhilarating.

The Beach Club has captured this with a splendid cuisine in finest culinary traditions.

Right here in the Rockaways

The Beach Club, a casual, family-themed dining and catering establishment, is one of Rockaway's most popular restaurants. The Beach Club stands adjacent to the Rockaway boardwalk overlooking the Atlantic Ocean and the beautiful Rockaway beach.

Kenny and Steve Good are your gracious hosts. They have been in the restaurant business in Rockaway for nearly 20 years and enjoy a wonderful relationship with the community. The Beach Club staff provides attentive professional service and makes every customer feel like part of the family. "We know most of our customers by name and if we don't, we try to learn them," says resident owner Kenny. The Beach Club offers something to please almost everyone's taste buds. Breakfast is served every day and a Grand Sunday Brunch features a giant smorgasbord to satisfy even the grandest of appetites. From hamburgers to Mexican specialties to pasta dishes and the finest steaks and seafood - you will have to agree that the menu selections are second to none. Kids love the Steeplechase Arcade and Boardwalk Sweet Shop. During the summer months, guests can dine outdoors on the ocean-view deck or in the Tiki Hut, an outdoor Polynesian-themed dining area and cocktail lounge and then stroll leisurely along the boardwalk. The Ocean Room, the Beach Club's private catering facility, offers an elegant setting for affairs from 30 to 200 people.

The decor is open and airy with tropical colors and palm trees. A special feature is a display of surfboards dating from the 1950's to the present along with a wonderful collection of vintage photographs and memorabilia from the early 1900's when Rockaway served as a major summer tourist destination for New York City. "People love to look back and remember the 'good old days' and think about the potential that Rockaway has for tourism in the future," adds Kenny. The Beach Club was built from ideas the Good brothers gathered in their travels combined with a touch of New York City. "Our idea was to take a little bit from each place we visited and bring it to Rockaway," explains Steve Good, Beach Club owner. "Rockaway has so much to offer and The Beach Club was designed to take advantage of it all." Located only 20 minutes from JFK Airport and less than an hour from Manhattan by ferry or car, Rockaway and The Beach Club offer a unique tourist destination you don't want to miss.

Phone: (718) 634-6500 • Fax: (718) 634-1884
www.thebeachclub.com

Breathtaking Photography . . .

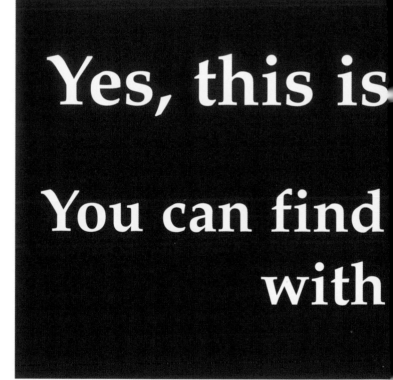

Yes, this is

You can find

with

Very Informative text . . .

New York.

it right here us.

Impressions in continuity

New York

1st Edition

After 125 Years
WE KNOW SOMETHING

FIREWORKS BY GRUCCI

photo by Mike Deutsch
WILDLIFE

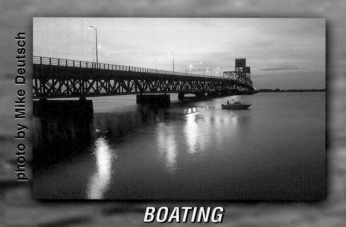
photo by Mike Deutsch
BOATING

photo by Mike Deutsch

Get Away
New York's Best

photo by Chris Jorge
Rockaway Artists Alliance inc.
PREMIERE OPENING
SAT. JUNE 10th 6pm to 8pm
SHOW RUNS
Movies
ARTS & CULTURE

photo by Jay Velasquez
SCU

For more information contact The Chamber of Commerce

●●● ABOUT SUMMER FUN!

BUILDING SAND CASTLES

photo by Kate Judge

To Rockaway
Kept Secret!

SUNSETS

photo by Mike Deutsch

SURFING

photo by Chris Jorge

photo by John J. Grillo

Less Than An Hour From Manhattan

DIVING

FISHING

of The Rockaways at 718-634-1300/rockawaychamberofcommerce.com

Donald W. Elliot Photography

www.dwestudios.com

A COLORFUL

CHANGE

OF PACE

AN APPETIZING CHANGE OF PACE
A culinary kaleidoscope of international cuisines. restaurants, cafes, bakeries and food shopping all within walking proximity of each other.

ASTORIA EMPORIA! Visit Steinway Street, "The Worlds Longest Department Store," along with the community's other shopping districts where you'll find plenty of unique shops and specialty boutiques.

AMERICAN MUSEUM OF THE MOVING IMAGE (AMMI), 718-784-0077. Tuesday–Friday NOON–5 P.M., Saturday and Sunday 11 A.M.–6 P.M.

ISAMU NOGUCHI GARDEN MUSEUM 718-204-7088. April–October, Wednesday–Friday 10 A.M.–5 P.M., Saturday and Sunday 11 A.M.–6 P.M.

SOCRATES SCULPTURE GARDEN 31-42 Vernon Boulevard. Open 10 A.M. to sunset.

BOHEMIAN HALL AND PARK (1910), 718-274-4925. Once there were more than 800 beer gardens in New York City. Now only Bohemian Hall remains, open weekends from Memorial Day through Labor Day.

For a FREE Visitor's Guide, Map, Calendar or general information call the Astoria Tourism Hotline at (718) 728-7922.

Funded in part by the NYC Department of Business Services

Central Astoria

LOCAL DEVELOPMENT COALITION INC.

HARLEM

"CORE OF THE APPLE... CREATIVE, BEAUTIFUL WITH CRAZY ENERGY... MESMERIZING..."

Harlem still stands in its historic building, not a physical façade, but a tribute to its rich history. A history that began with the Algonquin people, who first settled here, to a mixed race adventure with people from the Caribbean, who opened a trading post in 1613, ten years before the Dutch. Names of our Nation's founding fathers and famous early citizens such as Washington, Astor, Hamilton and Audubon - many of whom lived here - were closely associated with early Harlem. Always a melting pot, the 20th century opened up to the development of Harlem from a village of farms to country estates owned by New York's social elite. For more than a century, a prosperous middle class was proud to call it home.

The first and second world wars saw an increase in the number of African-Americans coming from the South, West Indies and Africa to Harlem seeking opportunities. It was from this migration that the Harlem Renaissance occurred. Within those thousands in search of a "better life" came the creative artists, writers and spokespersons that would define the period. James Van Der Zee photographed history-in-the-making, Duke Ellington played about it and Billy Holiday sang about it. Langston Hughes wrote about it and Zora Neale Thurston wrote to remind us of our southern roots. Paul Robeson's voice rang out with it here and abroad. Marcus Garvey, Martin Luther King, Jr., Malcolm X, and Adam Clayton Powell, Jr. orated from the streets of Harlem over the course of several decades from locations including the soapbox corner at 135th Street and Lenox Avenue, African Square on 125th Street and Seventh Avenue and in the churches. All these leaders were sources of inspiration to keep Americans moving forward in the face of racial and economic discrimination.

Many of these memories still stand as buildings but with new purposes - many were replaced and pose as new podiums in this, the Second Renaissance. The expression of those great artists and thinkers echoes through a new generation of eloquent spokespeople, artists, musicians, writers and business people whose contributions make Harlem among the most important communities of the 21st Century.

We are offering to you - residents and visitors - the Harlem USA2 map as a celebration to the resurgent Harlem Community and glorious Harlem past. The cultural institutions, restaurants, lounges, businesses, schools and places of worship on this map are the essences of Harlem for you to enjoy. With this map you can navigate through the Harlem of yesterday, today and tomorrow.

Harlem USA2, a revitalized version of the original Harlem USA map produced in 1987, celebrates the new millennium renaissance of the cultural artistic, entertainment, and now, economic mecca of the world.

NuJAPPLE MARKETING INC.

102-104 West 124th Street, New York, NY 10027 tel: 212.932.2737 fax: 212.678.5018 www.harlemusamap.com

The Albany City Trolley
e³ Visitors Center

The Albany Visitors Center

A unique location for your wedding
or
private party

The Albany City Trolley

Comfortable seating for 28 adults

❧

2001 Dates Available, April-October

 25 Quackenbush Sq. | Albany, New York 12207 | 518-434-0405

Albany Is...

Albany County Convention and Visitors Bureau

25 Quackenbush Square,
Albany, NY 12207
(518) 434-1217
(800) 258 3582

The Perfect Summer Vacation Destination

Take a moment and discover why Albany has been welcoming visitors for almost four centuries. Begin at the Albany Heritage Area Visitors Center . . . this summer we're offering orientation shows, walking tours, ever-changing exhibits, the Henry Hudson planetarium and trolley tours of Albany's downtown and its historic homes.

Stop in at the NYS Museum to view the Indian long house and the Cohoes Mastodon; the State Capitol with its million dollar staircase and the restored legislative chambers. Enjoy the fabulous modern art collection along the Empire State Plaza and take a side trip to visit our historic homes like Cherry Hill, Ten Broeck and Schuyler mansions.

Or, just lie back and enjoy the mighty Hudson as it flows past on its way to the sea. **Call 1-800-258-3582.**

www.albany.org

I ♥ NY

The State House

M O R G A N

WELCOME TO
THE MORGAN STATE HOUSE
Downtown Albany

VOTED BEST IN THE
CAPITAL & SARATOGA REGION

The Morgan State House is a superb example of late nineteenth century American Aesthetic design. The life-long home and studio of the noted American artist and suffragette Alice Morgan Wright (1881-1975), it has been completely restored into the most unique accommodations in the Capital District.

One-of-a-kind Historic Rowhouse Mansion

19TH
CENTURY
CHARM & ELEGANCE

The Guest Suites

The State House Morgan and Washington Park are both ideal for introducing your clients and guests to the charm and ambiance of downtown Albany.

The guest rooms and apartment suites are individually designed and handsomely furnished. In the European Tradition, our Beds are our signature. Feather mattresses, down comforters and soft cotton sheets provide the ultimate nights rest.

For those staying longer periods of time, our apartment suites are ideal.

WELCOME TO A PLACE OF COMFORT AND PRIVACY

393 STATE STREET
ALBANY, NEW YORK 12210
LOCAL
518 · 427 · 6063
TOLL FREE
888 · 427 · 6063
WWW.STATEHOUSE.COM

Receptions & Special Events

Our facility is intimate enough for small meetings and conferences and yet can comfortably accommodate 50 people on the mansion's main floor. Our professional staff will take care of every detail.

So many places to visit
So many memories to share

We are here for you.

Getaway Travel & Sightseeing Tours

3257 45th Street, Long Island City, New York, USA 11103
Mailing Address: P.O. Box 770338 Woodside, NY 11377
(718) 639-2668 • (718) 956-4110 • Fax (718) 639-2890
E-mail: TMScorpio@aol.com • www.getawaysightseeing.bizland.com

List of Illustrations

Whitney Museum of American Art

1.) Alexander Calder
<u>Calder's Circus</u>   1926-1931
Mixed media: wire, wood, metal, cloth, yarn,
paper, cardboard, leather, string, rubber
tubing, corks, buttons, rhinestones, pipe
cleaners, bottle caps

Dimensions variable, overall: 54 x 94 ¼ x 94 ¼ in.
                                 (137.2 x 239.4 x 239.4 cm.)

Accessories overall: 76 ½ x 97 ¾ x 96 ¾ in.
                                 (194.3 x 248.3 x 245.7 cm.)

2.) Willem deKooning
<u>Woman and Bicycle</u>   1952-1953
Oil on canvas
76 ½ x 49 in. (194.3 x 124.5 cm.)
Collection of Whitney Museum of American Art
Purchase

© 2000 Willem deKooning Revocable Trust / Artists Rights Society(ARS), New York

3.) Richard Diebenkorn
<u>Girl Looking at Landscape</u>   1957
Oil on canvas
59 x 60 3/8 in. (149.9 x 153.4 cm.)
Collection of Whitney Museum of American Art
Gift of Mr. and Mrs. Alan H. Temple

4.) Robert Henri
<u>Gertrude Vanderbilt Whitney</u>   1916
Oil on canvas
50 x 72 in. (127 x 182.9 cm.)
Collection of Whitney Museum of American Art
Gift of Flora Whitney Miller

5.) Elie Nadelman
Tango   ca. 1919
Painted cherry wood and gesso
3 units, overall: 35 ⅞ x 26 x 13 ⅞ in.
                            (91.1 x 66 x 35.2 cm.)
Collection of Whitney Museum of American Art Purchase

6.) Joseph Stella
The Brooklyn Bridge: Variation on an Old Theme   1939
Oil on canvas
70 x 42 in. (177.S x 106.7 cm.)
Collection of Whitney Museum of American Art
Purchase

7.) Reginald Marsh
Twenty Cent Movie, 1936
Egg tempera on composition board
30 x 40 in. (76.2 x 101.6 cm.)
Collection of Whitney Museum of American Art

8.) Lee Bronson, Underpass.
October 29, 1999 - March17, 2000
Whitney Museum of American Art at Philip Morris
Photo by: George Hirose

9.) Leonard & Evelyn Lauder Gallery
Robert Henri, Gaston Lachaise, Maurice Prendergast,
George Bellows, Gertrude Vanderbilt Whitney

10.) Richard Diebenkorn
Girl looking at Landscape, 1957
Oil on canvas
59 x 60 3/8 in. (149.9 x 153.4 cm.)
Collection of Whitney Museum of American Art
Gift of Mr. and Mrs. Alan H. Temple
Purchase

The Jewish Museum

Smithsonian National Museum of the American Indian

1.) Jolene Rickard, Reservation X

2.) C. Maxx Stevens, Reservation X

3.) Marianne Nicolson, Reservation X

4.) Mary Longman, Reservation X

5.) Seed Gathering Basket, Hupa, Ca

6.) Shelly Niro, Reservation X

7.) Cradleboard, Yuma, Az

8.) F. Kabotie, Hopi, Snake Dance

9.) Bark Mask, Tierra del Fuego

Best of
Impressions in continuity
New York

An International Publication of
Sorrell Communications Inc.
New York, USA

Publishers
Victoria B. Mascetta • Nicholas D. Mascetta

Executive Editor
Edward Wallis Doucet

Associate Editor
Luis Miguel B. Arcangel

Creative Art Director
Ryan L. Bouie

Photo Editor
Don Riepe

Writers
Allison Caalim • Marivic Cuizon • Aileen Caalim

Account Managers
Jenna Belic • Calista Nanton

Editorial Assistants
Naimah Smalls • Brenda Ali • Mary Maltese

Production Assistant
Tahir Brown

Contributing Writers
Darlene Frenette • Carla Moran

Creative Consultants
Morris Berman • Charles Kuhtic

Editorial Consultants
Elizabeth Sulik • Cory Reed • Thelma Hiland
Lourdes Villa • Tess M. Cabadin

Contributing Photographers
Peter Aaron/Esto • Diane Shapiro • Bill Meng • Dennis De Mello
Kate Judge • Bart Barlow • Winnie Klotz • Judy Lawne • John Uher
Peter Medilek • Sinichiro Inoue • Bruno Hausch • Patrick Rytikangas

Internet Consultant
Vincent Villa

Website Design
Network Solutions by Frank Semeraro
website: http//www.fsemeraro.com • email: webmaster@fsemeraro.com

Sorrell Communications Inc.
79-06 31 Avenue, East Elmhusrt, New York 11370
Telephone: (718) 205-0665 • Facsimile: (718) 205-1061
www.sorrellthebestof.com • email: sorrellcom@aol.com

Best of

Impressions in continuity

New York

Best of *Impressions in continuity*
New York

Sorrell Communications Inc.
79-06 31st. Avenue, East Elmhusrt, New York 11370
Telephone: (718) 205-0665 • Facsimile: (718) 205-1061
www.sorrellthebestof.com - e-mail: sorrellcomm@aol.com

Will you please send me _____ copy/copies at US$ 75.00 each.
(Add US$10.00 postage and handling per book for overseas orders).
I enclose check / money order in US$ _____

Name _____

Address _____

City _____ State _____ Zip _____ Country _____

Tel. Nos. _____ Fax No. _____ E-mail _____

Best of *Impressions in continuity*
New York

Sorrell Communications Inc.
79-06 31st. Avenue, East Elmhusrt, New York 11370
Telephone: (718) 205-0665 • Facsimile: (718) 205-1061
www.sorrellthebestof.com - e-mail: sorrellcomm@aol.com

Will you please send me _____ copy/copies at US$ 75.00 each.
(Add US$10.00 postage and handling per book for overseas orders).
I enclose check / money order in US$ _____

Name _____

Address _____

City _____ State _____ Zip _____ Country _____

Tel. Nos. _____ Fax No. _____ E-mail _____

Best of *Impressions in continuity*
New York

Sorrell Communications Inc.
79-06 31st. Avenue, East Elmhusrt, New York 11370
Telephone: (718) 205-0665 • Facsimile: (718) 205-1061
www.sorrellthebestof.com - e-mail: sorrellcomm@aol.com

Will you please send me _____ copy/copies at US$ 75.00 each.
(Add US$10.00 postage and handling per book for overseas orders).
I enclose check / money order in US$ _____

Name _____

Address _____

City _____ State _____ Zip _____ Country _____

Tel. Nos. _____ Fax No. _____ E-mail _____

Best of *Impressions in continuity*
New York

Sorrell Communications Inc.
79-06 31st. Avenue, East Elmhusrt, New York 11370
Telephone: (718) 205-0665 • Facsimile: (718) 205-1061
www.sorrellthebestof.com - e-mail: sorrellcomm@aol.com

Will you please send me _____ copy/copies at US$ 75.00 each.
(Add US$10.00 postage and handling per book for overseas orders).
I enclose check / money order in US$ _____

Name _____

Address _____

City _____ State _____ Zip _____ Country _____

Tel. Nos. _____ Fax No. _____ E-mail _____

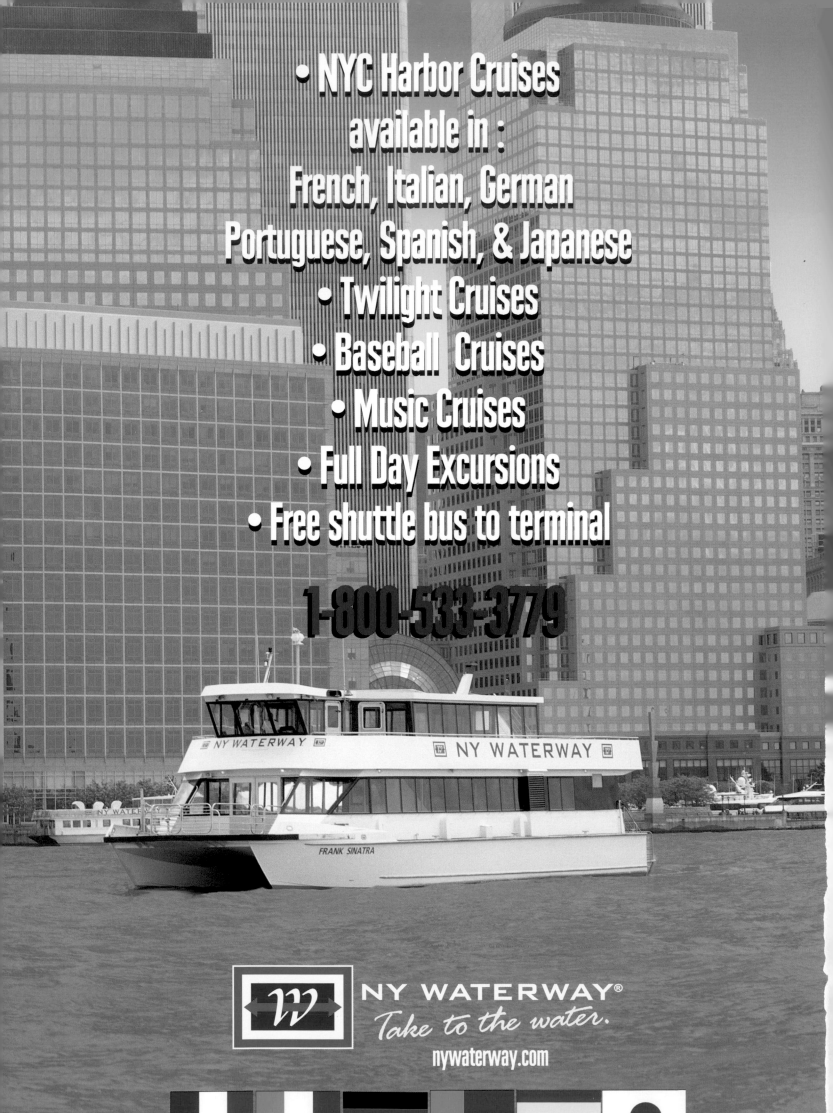